Table of Contents

Part One

Part Two

Introduction

The true purpose of religion is nothing less than the awakening of human beings to a vivid and transforming consciousness of spiritual reality. Change, or better yet, metamorphosis, is the goal of religion and of life, two words that I believe are ultimately synonymous. This change moves us toward new forms of behavior and introduces us to a radically new understanding of ourselves and of others. It especially leads us into a moment by moment awareness of our connectedness to all creation.

In spite of their rich history of illumined individuals who manifested that unbounded universal love so central to the great teachings, religious institutions of all faiths often inhibit the possibility of such development. By identifying the barriers, I hope to assist you in encountering the real *meat*, or to put it in more traditional terms, the *living bread* that empowers us to experience the presence of the divine in the here and now.

To speak of spiritual transformation suggests a study of all of the forms generated by culture, history and revelation. From tribal myths to the sophisticated teachings of Sufism, from the *Advaita* of Hinduism to the *Tao* of Chinese mystics, nearly every manifestation of the religious impulse presents us with regenerating insights into the nature of reality at the most intimate levels of our existence.

This book will not cover the vast landscape of world religions. Experts like Mircea Eliade and Joseph Campbell have provided us with masterful and encyclopedic works on the matter. The focus here is on the Western world and more specifically on one of its central driving forces, Christianity. We will observe this particular form taken by the religious impulse from two perspectives: 1) as a case study of how structured and externalized spiritual teachings can suffocate the truth inherent in their original formulation; 2) as an exploration of a particular faith for the purpose of uncovering its unique contributions to spiritual evolution that are universal in their application.

For certain readers, the issue of the Church's mishandling of spiritual knowledge will seem obvious. Many seekers of meaning have long ago left behind the dogmas and old forms of this splintered organization. The following pages will point out that in rejecting the outer form, they may have thrown out the true content as well, to the detriment of any genuine seeker of spiritual transformation.

In this age of hunger for meaning, it is incumbent upon persons driven by a need to encounter the sacred to find that which is universal and practical at the core of all religious teachings. A Tibetan Buddhist can be enriched by the wisdom of the Christ just as a Christian can develop a deeper inner practice through a study of Islamic mysticism.

Our epoch can no longer accept the artificial walls that have stood for centuries between peoples and cultures. This is a new age and there is no going back. The validity of religion is now measured by its value to human development, not by a rigid belief system that is used as a battering ram against other groups. Nor is a merely social program enough to satisfy the thirst for God.

The criteria for identifying the worth of religious teachings—beneath the crust of history and the weight of institutions—is found in their ability to transform a self-centered nature into one that is radiant with compassion. Each of us is meant to come face to face with the depths of our being and awaken to our greatest fulfillment: becoming conscious children of the universe, incarnating the unconditional love that created us all.

This work is divided into two parts. Part One depicts the early appearances of religious expression in the first civilizations and in Hebrew wisdom. This study documents the fact that religion has always dealt specifically with inner awakening to the presence of the sacred. It then goes on to cover the tensions between institutionalized religion and spiritual growth as found in contemporary Christianity.

Part Two investigates the inner meaning of the teachings and the experiential significance of their primary practices. Practical methods are then presented for application in daily life. They are synthesized from traditional, esoteric, and eastern sources that have long proven the power of the transforming process emphasized throughout this book.

Every religion is a treasure map. History, human error and institutional structures have often mistaken the map for the treasure, thereby forgetting its true intent. This book is a tool for digging up the treasure that will "set us free." My aim is to assist you in those efforts. The central claim of this work is found in its title: it is in our hearts, the center of our being, that the treasure is found.

These last years of the twentieth century cry out for a holistic appropriation of the teachings of the past that will metamorphosize the human soul. It is my hope that the reader will find here the means for penetrating to the heart of the religious purpose, recognizing the failures and distortions of its visible expressions, and uniting with the inner truth that makes us one.

My journey could well have led me into an abyss of confusion and despair were it not for the encounter with my soul mate, Rebecca, who appeared at a critical crossroad and is now my beloved wife and companion on the way. I wish all seekers the grace of this unfathomable mystery.

May this book assist you on your pilgrimage toward transforming Truth.

PART ONE

I will put my law within them, and I will write it upon their hearts.

Jeremiah 31:33

I

Religion and Personal Transformation

Life is not a factory in which we work until we drop. Life is a sacred gift through which we have the possibility of uniting with the true purpose of our coming into being. But no one can tell us to rejoice or be grateful. Such feelings can only come spontaneously from our own unique way of living. This is our birthright: that we each become our true, free selves, able to rejoice in the gift of life.

RELIGION

A rediscovery of the Divine in the midst of life will enlighten enough minds to alter the dangerous course of human ignorance, greed and violence. This is the true role of religion. Religion ought to provide the opportunity for us to become aware of the nature of our world, and to thereby discover how we fit into that world and what contribution we might make. It should not be a mere reflection of a particular cultural worldview, but ought rather to offer an understanding different from the one provided by the mores and priorities of a secular and materialistic culture.

Religion means to "re-link" with that which is greater than we are, with our true identity and purpose. But the word "religion" is stained with bloodshed, intolerance, half-truths, and self-righteousness. Meanwhile, thousands of people, millions perhaps, are seeking meaning and direction, and in doing so have turned away from institutionalized religion. The primary reason is that these seekers are in need of an experiential discovery of the contents of the teachings.

EXPERIENCE

We have all known moments in our lives when we were overwhelmed by something out of the ordinary. Stimulated by wonder, joy, fear, or beauty, these moments are more than emotional experiences. There is something about them that is indefinable and deeply spiritual. They may fill us with healing inner peace, unlike anything we have ever known, or with certainty and courage. Even as children, something within us recognized that we were caught up in momentous encounters.

These brief moments of vaster consciousness free us from our anxieties, release us from captivity to our narrow sense of self and flood us with life-giving acceptance and understanding. We generally live in a psychological cocoon created by imitation, fear, imagination. When we escape this prison, we find the fulfillment of our deepest desires. The great mystics pointed out that at the root of all our desires is the one Desire—to unite with the sacred.

Rather than attempting to identify the nature of this

desire, I will leave that to each one's discovery and encounter. Instead, I will focus on the means to prepare the ground, to toil in our inner field so that we might become capable of experiencing and manifesting the spiritual depths of life. In order to accomplish this, I will begin by sharing my own experiences.

A good deal of my childhood was spent in Europe, and I was often taken to cathedrals and monasteries. It was in these places that I came upon the sense of "sacred space" or more specifically, that quality of silence in which one comes in contact with otherworldliness. The following is a passage from one of my journals:

I felt the ancient dampness chill me to the bone. Never before had I experienced so strongly the presence of an invisible universe populated with beings who transcended space and time. They were more real to me than the artifacts that loomed in the shadows. I had been told that kings and bishops were buried in the crypt beneath my feet. Now the feeling of my own mortality rose into my awareness for the first time and placed me squarely before the very mystery of my existence.

In the center of the sanctuary, multi-colored sunrays broke through the darkness. I looked up at the stained-glass windows, instinctively seeking comfort from the high places brilliant with sunlight. The impassive faces of the saints stared back at me. And beyond them, the giant image of the Christ, holding up his right hand in a sign of blessing to the world. I felt a strange, wondrous relief fill my soul as I looked into the gentle eyes of the great icon. The face of the Son of God drew me in with a magnetic power I had never known before.

A profound, measureless peace came over me. The tension in my body melted under the mystic warmth of the Divine Presence. I stared unblinking at the image of the Christ which was inexplicably healing me like the warm embrace of my mother. Time vanished as I basked in a glow of unconditional love raining down upon me from the very heart of the cosmos. The blessing of the Logos painted on the ancient window vibrated through my being with greater power than any feeling I had ever encountered.

I intuitively knew that from this day on I would never again feel completely abandoned or lost in hopelessness. The mysterious presence of this life-giving Love would always be there, even without my awareness of it.

Later, these moments occurred at very difficult times in my life. In my early twenties, I lived in Paris trying to jump-start a career, and I knew quite well the meaning of the term "alone in the crowd." It was Christmas eve and I was far from family, friends, and home.

I was walking to the subway and found myself glancing up at the black sky above which was peppered with countless stars. All of a sudden, a surge of deep joy flooded my soul. Inexplicably, the shimmering stars so far away gave me a sense of not being alone, of fitting into some greater plan, of unconditional acceptance and trust that everything would be all right even though my circumstances seemed so ominous. At the very heart of my isolation and at its most painful moment, I found myself in an oasis of peace and healing.

I was able to carry on another six months after that experience until a turning point came along and brought me into a new phase of my journey. That brief instant on a cold winter night was enough to keep me going through times of desperation.

TRANSFORMATION

Transformation is the overcoming of self-centeredness that leads us into another relationship to reality. It introduces us to an ability to love unconditionally, to develop real compassion, or *objective love* as some have called it. This is the goal and purpose of all true religious teachings.

Transformation leads us into an experience of life that takes into account its invisible dimension. This is not merely an intellectual exercise but includes our senses as well. One of the great guides through these numinous experiences is the German psychotherapist and spiritual master Karlfried Graf Dürckheim. His teachings are presented in a later chapter as he is so central to the effort of pragmatic inner transformation. His insight on the role of the senses in spiritual encounter is of great significance to all seekers, as is evident in the following passage taken from *Dialogue on the Path of Initiation.*

We should take seriously certain experiences of being. They are of two kinds: the little "touches" of Being and the great liberating experiences. At the heart of every event in this world, we can be touched by a reality that has nothing to do with the world: it is another dimension that transcends the usual horizon of our consciousness. We are suddenly seized from within by something that gives to all that is interior or exterior, to the whole ambiance of our actual state, a particular quality that we call "numinous." These are singular moments where we can feel another life within us and in all that surrounds us, the life of essential Being. The feeling that invades us in those moments can be fascinating, liberating or terrifying, but we always feel the fullness of Being that attracts us. In order to open ourselves to this experience, which is available in every moment, we must first develop a particular attitude which orients our whole person. We then encounter in everything another being and not merely a thing. Whatever the shape of the encounter: a simple color, a sound, an aroma, an object, a countryside, even an abstract concept, we are always called by a "you" through all that touches us.(1)

Religion has always dealt with radical change in human beings. But over time, it was obscured by various factors that will be described in the following pages. We cannot blame this degeneration entirely on power-hungry tyrants or intolerant fanatics. We generate our own veils, covering reality as it truly is. Attachment, identification, "maya" all refer to the filters that we place over the mind's eye. Yet we are so much more than we imagine ourselves to be. Life is a spiritual adventure, not the daily grind to pay our bills that we know so well.

In this chapter we examine the first civilizations in order to make the case for the impact that myth and religion had on the human psyche. It is the psyche and its awakening that are critical here, not rituals, symbols or any other external phenomena, for they are only means to an end. We will also explore the world of the Hebrew prophets who are the background for the Judeo-Christian religion that has shaped Western culture. Again we will see that their pronouncements were not simply rules and obligations handed down from on high, and certainly not visions of future events foretold for our time. They were expressions of encounters with the sacred and were meant to lead their people to that same experience.

Finally, we will complete this study with a reflection on the message of Jeremiah who was the first Hebrew prophet to formulate the ideas that are central to this book. He was the one to announce that the Holy One, the "I Am" of Creation had inscribed in the human heart the way of return to our original unity.

THE FIRST SPARKS OF RELIGION

The excavations in the barren soil of the Near East have unearthed fragments of walls and traces of foundations from the sacred temples of Babylon, Kish, Nineveh, and ancient Ur. Faded carvings and shattered tablets are the last witnesses to a way of life that placed religion at the center of existence. We can only wonder at the impact these great structures had on the human spirit, for they were designed to be places of encounter between cosmic powers and human beings.

These temples towered over cities for three thousand years, vibrating with centuries of devoted worship. Beyond the gates and courtyards, approached only by the high priests after performing solemn rites of purification, stood the inner sanctum that harbored the image of the deity. The civilization's finest works of art lay hidden in these secluded places. They were not decorations but rather perpetuated an attitude of prayer and thanksgiving. But these "high places" were in no way removed from the rhythm of daily life. For instance, many Mesopotamian hymns were concerned with the alleviation of human suffering, and carried overtones of personal relationships with the gods. Harps, tambourines, flutes, and lyres were used to induce high emotional states. Scholars have also discovered that Sumerian, Babylonian, and Assyrian physicians knew of the hallucinatory effects of certain plants. Though they were used primarily for healing, they may have been ingested to achieve experiences of the sacred.

The remnants of these bygone cultures are faint shadows of an intense presence of the numinous among societies deeply aware of their own position in the hierarchy of universal powers. The vivid wonder before the forces of nature and the reliance on their patterns for the survival of their agricultural world created a humility and gratitude that lifted these ancient peoples into an instinctive awareness of human frailty and transience. Their attention was focused on the holy dimensions of existence that we modern people have virtually eradicated from our psyche.

MYTHICAL EXPERIENCE

In attempting to grasp some quality of the mythical or religious experience in its immediate and urgent impact on the human spirit, we need to take the advice of those who have given the major portion of their lives to the penetration of these ancient mysteries. Theodor Gaster insists that personal participation is vital to any understanding of myth. Myth begins with the social relationship to a Being, not intellectual subscription to a concept. Dr. C. Kerenyi, an associate of C.G. Jung, suggests that we have lost our immediate feeling for the great realities of the spirit to which all true mythology belongs, and he wonders whether experience of mythology is still possible for the children of this age.(2)

Awakening an understanding which will plunge some 4000 years back into our ancestry necessitates a flexibility and subtlety of thought which, as the great anthropologist Thorkild Jacobsen observes, will perceive interrelations of concepts that are frequently incongruent with anything in our present-day culture and outlook. And Ernst Cassirer, one of the monumental minds to have dedicated himself to these studies, asserts that some act of emotion is necessary in deciphering the content of a myth's religious teaching.(3) Our effort to understand the truth of myths must be guided by the realization that the mentality of ancient peoples did not invent myths but *experienced* them. Mircea Eliade believes that myth becomes decadent and obscured when it is turned into a mere tale or legend. He tells us:

There is no myth which is not the unveiling of a "mystery," the revelation of a primordial event which inaugurated either a constituent structure of reality or a kind of human behavior.(4)

For the societies of the Ancient Near East, myth was the only valid revelation of reality, a reality which made persons aware of themselves and the physical universe as part of an encompassing whole. This awareness is an entryway into a life in which "one ceases to exist in the everyday world and enters a transfigured, auroral world impregnated with the supernatural 'presence'."(5)

The primordial mysteries became accessible to the worshiper through an exalted state of being that struck the deepest chords of his spirit. This is the dimension which Jung labeled the "collective unconscious." Out of this experience can come an inner state of harmony and integration taking place on a cosmic scale of consciousness.

That a special 'ear' is needed for it (myth), just as for music or poetry, is obvious. Here as well 'ear' means resonance, a sympathetic passing out of oneself.(6)

Myths drew men and women into a deep awareness of their participation in a sacred cosmic order in which the gods, the natural world, and society blended into one another. Jacobsen observes that by representing the forces of nature as anthropomorphic gods, and telling stories about their relationships in terms of human psychology, the Sumerians (who left behind the oldest traces of mythology) were able to understand and accept the workings of the natural world in a manner that would have been impossible on a purely logical and descriptive basis.(7) It is this unique experience of confrontation with power not of this world that made myths "vehicles of true religious response."(8)

MYTH AND HUMAN IDENTITY

The Mesopotamians understood that the events described in their primordial stories were the foundation of their lives. The world and humankind exist because supernatural beings had exercised creative powers in the "beginning." Beneath the formalities of ritual were genuine requests for personal human-divine relationships. Though the ancients tended to think of themselves in terms of communal relationships and existed by virtue of belonging to a group, the religious experience of the individual in the presence of a supernatural power reflected a clear manifestation of the search for self. The four protective spirits in Mesopotamian culture are considered by some scholars as individualized and mythologized carriers of certain specific psychological aspects of the personality as it relates the ego to the outside world.

Identity was intimately connected with names. The name of a god constituted a real part of his essence and efficacy, designating the sphere of energies within which each deity acted. Image and word were endowed with power. Until the rise of personal gods, the identity of the individual was enmeshed with that of the community. Myth transformed existence into dynamic experience. The mythological process deals with nothing less than the very forces out of which consciousness came into being. Ernst Cassirer tells us that myth is "the odyssey of the pure consciousness of God."(9)

In our sophistication, we have gained much protection from the gods of lightning, wind and darkness, but we have lost that deeper communion with the wonder of the cosmic harmony that dances eternally within us and in the outside world.

Modern self-sufficiency and presumption have lifted frail humanity to heights where it does not belong. Many of our contemporaries can only hope to live in forgetfulness of the devastation awaiting their self-centered universe, whereas the ancient myths did not speak of annihilation ahead but rather revealed the way toward a passage into another form. Mortality was a fluid movement in the sacred patterns of Being. It is to this state of commingling with the vaster consciousness of the powers of Creation that the serene figures of ancient Mesopotamia point.

For our purposes here—uncovering the essence of the religious impulse—we turn from these first manifestations to the formulations of a particular people, the Hebrews. Though they called themselves "the Chosen People" and made a unique contribution to humanity, the source of their teaching begins in a wider arena that connects them to the universal vision of all the great religious teachings.

EGYPTIAN INFLUENCES

One of the most critical links between various religions, revealing that the truth they teach is the same, is seen in the little known fact that Hebrew spiritual knowledge originated in the teachings of ancient Egypt. This assertion would tie the teachings of the Torah to the source of all the primary streams of esoteric knowledge available to humanity. Egypt was the location of the great library of Alexandria and the center of esoteric schools that attracted the likes of Plato. This oneness of Truth is a most compelling idea in our day and age when the reality of the global community and our interconnection across all nations and cultures is an obvious daily event. It carries the seeds of reconciliation, understanding and peace for our tormented world. Our work is to find the keys to the meaning of these ancient teachings that reveal the universal truth which sets us free.

The sacred wisdom of the Hebrews clearly dates back to more ancient sources. This connection is no longer merely the opinion of metaphysical organizations, but proven by modern biblical scholarship to be true. A classic example of this phenomenon is found in Psalm 104, the famous "pearl of the Psalter." Scholars point out that, despite its parallels with Genesis 1, the psalm does not show dependence on the story of creation. It excels Genesis 1 in richness of imagination and is an older version dating from the time when the sagas of Genesis and Exodus were still in the process of flux and growth, not having as yet received their fixed literary form.

Scholars tell us that Psalm 104 is not an original composition by a Hebrew psalmist but is derived from and owes its magnificent spirit to the Hymn to the Sun attributed to Pharaoh Ikhnaton (Amenhotep IV, 1375-1358 B.C.). The noted Egyptologist Hugo Gressmann observed that, in their ideas about God and the intimate relationship that human beings may cultivate with their Creator, the Egyptians of the Eighteenth and Nineteenth Dynasties were far in advance of the Hebrews of the early monarchical period. Such ideas did not prevail to any extent until the latter half of the eighth century B.C., in the time of Amos, Isaiah and Hezekiah. The opportunity for becoming acquainted with Egyptian thought and literature was never lacking in Israel. The two countries had commercial and political ties, and maintained friendly relations down to 586 B.C. when the Hebrews were forced into exile. At the time of the Deuteronomic legislation (622 B.C.), Egyptians must have lived in considerable numbers in Israel since Deuteronomy 23:8f. states that third generation Egyptians may be admitted to the community of Yahweh.

It is well known that for nearly two millennia Egypt exercised a powerful influence over Palestine. The two cultures intermingled to such an extent that hundreds of Hebrew loan words are found in the Egyptian of the New Kingdom. King Solomon married an Egyptian princess (I Kings 9:15f.) and Moses reached a place of considerable social importance in Egypt. The scholar W.F. Albright suggests that Moses' original Torah may well have contained Egyptian elements that were later integrated with native Hebrew conceptions. Moreover, Moses introduced to his people the ancient Egyptian custom of circumcision that was practiced for at least three thousand years by the Nile dwellers.

The fact that Moses adopted as a universal distinguishing mark of the Israelites a sacred Egyptian practice is evidence that he was drawing upon his knowledge of Egyptian religion. Acts 7:22 tells us that Moses was instructed in all the wisdom of the Egyptians.

Among the major influences that can be traced back to Egyptian sources are:

1. The concept of the god who is the sole creator of everything and the formula by which his name is derived ("Who causes to be what comes into existence," which is used repeatedly in the Hymn to Amon, 15th century B.C.).

2. The concept of a single god and the establishment of a doctrine based on monotheism.

3. The recognition of a universal cosmic dominion of the deity.

Furthermore, Moses' Torah translates as "teaching," a word used exclusively in the slightly earlier system known as *sbayet* (teaching) originated by Ikhnaton. Through the medium of Semitic scribes who studied Egyptian and learned their trade in the Egyptian writing-schools, many of the ideas and literary artifices contained in poems of the Eighteenth and Nineteenth Dynasties passed into Palestine. Extracts of these works may have begun to filter into Palestine even before the reign of Hezekiah, who initiated the re-copying of Egyptian poems and treatises that may well have stimulated the reform movement in Judah.

Egyptian influence penetrated Hebrew thought to such an extent that we find its influence even in the New Testament. In the myth of Isis, who was known as the mother of God, her divine child Horus is miraculously conceived and born in a stable!

THE UNIVERSAL TEACHING OF IKHNATON

The young pharaoh Ikhnaton inspired a universalism not
found before in the three thousand years of Egyptian
religion. He attempted to create a world religion and
displaced not only the inherent nationalism in Egyptian
religion, but all the gods as well in favor of a single, universal
god, the Aton. Ikhnaton was the first individual we know of
in history to shape his times by rejecting the sordidness of
religion and the indecent wealth and lavish rituals of the
temples. Some scholars suggest that he was the first person
to understand rightly the meaning of divinity. For instance,
Ikhnaton forbade his artists from making images of Aton on
the grounds that the true God has no form.

He understood God as a life-giving intangible essence.
The symbol of Aton (the sun disc from which diverging
beams radiate downward, each ending in a human hand), was
not worshipped. Rather, the divinity was the power that
produced and sustained the energy of the sun. This Solar
theology was closely identified with the development of the
moral consciousness of Egypt. Aton was to be found not in
battles and victories, but in flowers and trees, in all forms of
life and growth. The divinity was the creative and nourishing
heat of the sun that gives life to all that exists. With this
depiction of the deity, Ikhnaton formulated the profound
idea of God's immanence, the presence of the divine within
matter and, specifically, in human form. For the first time in
history, God was conceived as a formless being. Ikhnaton's

god was an intangible essence, the energetic force that acted through the sun, the creator who held all things in his hands. He was both transcendent and immanent, original causation and continuous presence. The omnipresence and beneficence of the sun evolved into an understanding of Aton as a compassionate mother-father of creation. There was no mention of hatred, jealousy or wrath, of hell or of judgment of God, for Aton was called "the Lord of Love."

THE WISDOM OF THE HEBREW PEOPLE

Investigating the understanding of an ancient people requires a radical release of presuppositions imposed upon us by our own culture. Since the human soul is the stage upon which we witness the entrance of "personal religion," it is necessary to understand how the soul was perceived among the Hebrews in the Ancient Near East.

Quite contrary to the modern concept, the Hebrews did not consider the soul to be a thinking organism. For them the human soul was a "depth of forces."(10) Its fathomless powers flooded individuals with new understanding of their obligations to their God and to their community. The total being of the person became involved in the apprehension of truth. For the Israelite, thinking was not the solving of abstract problems. Thinking did not entail premises and conclusions, but rather a grasp of totality. Knowledge, therefore, meant familiarity of the most intimate kind. The "knowledge of God" mentioned in the Old Testament was not simply absorption by the mind of accurate theological information, but the involvement of a person with a Person.

The great philosopher Martin Buber called it an "I - Thou" encounter. The life of the human being was open to God at every moment, undivided by opposing spheres called the religious and the secular. Life was understood as the happiness and expansion of the soul. Even a stone was seen as an organism with peculiar forces of a certain mysterious capacity.

THE PROPHETS

The Hebrew prophets were distinguished from other people by a peculiar psychic or spiritual development often expressed by trances and fits. This was the foundation for the common people's reverence toward them, and the prophet's own conviction that he was set apart from others.

Certain features of the prophetic writings do seem to point to an intensity of psychic experience. This accessibility to influences other than those acting through ordinary sense organs was universally recognized by the Hebrews. The prophets had immediate experience of God.

ECSTATIC STATES

The violent movements of the soul, exemplified in ecstatic trances, obliterated the consciousness of self and created an entrance for the message and presence of the holy. These states were an expression of the soul's ability to transcend itself and connect beyond its limits with the Divine, establishing a certain kinship between the Hebrew prophets and the Christian mystics. The experience of the prophets might well be ascribed by the modern mind to illusions of the senses, dual personality, or some other subjective phenomenon. But, for the Hebrews, these experiences were direct and unmistakable communications from Yahweh. They understood the "ruach" (breath) of Yahweh as a potent influence that could create new conditions within human nature. It was the link between the individual and God.

Through his own ruach, that is, through his conscious life viewed in its highest possibilities, he was in touch with the ruach of God, the source of humanity's greatest achievements.(11)

The Hebrews did not live in the limited three-dimensional world where we create separations that are simply illusions of the senses. The sacred broke through time, space, and matter at every point.

THE PROPHET OF THE INNER LAW

Jeremiah is generally regarded as the first prophet to introduce intimacy in the religious life of the Hebrews. From his profound spiritual perception came that great step in the history of religion that turned it from the formalism of an external worship to a discovery of God within the heart of every person. He made known the true intent of religion:

And no longer shall each man teach his neighbor and each his brother, saying, "Know the Lord," for they shall all know me, from the least of them to the greatest, says the Lord. (Jeremiah 31:34)

Jeremiah has been called by some the "father of

mystics." Born into an old priestly family around 640 B.C., he lived through the destruction of Jerusalem in 587 B.C. and the subsequent massive exile of his people. Though a naturally timid man, his sense of a divine mission led him to confront the superficial prophets of his day and the general immorality of his people. He was rejected for his relentless integrity and uncompromising outcries. He is thought to have died in exile in Egypt.

With Jeremiah came a movement toward a clarification of the prophetic consciousness that pointed to a higher level of religion. In his forty years of anguished struggle, Jeremiah saw the need for radical change in individuals if God's will was to be done in Israel. He focused on the necessity for purity of heart.

> He gains a glimpse of the truth that the pure in heart alone can see God, and that only through what is Godlike in man are God's mind and purpose discerned.(12)

The prophetic vocation became the center of a new, intimate relationship between the human and the divine in the mysterious depths of the soul. Only Jeremiah, of all the prophets, dared to converse with God in a fully human, personal way. In his laments, prayers, and tears, he opened the way for an encounter in which the transient communicated directly with the eternal.

He became aware that, whatever painful outward experiences he endured, knowing God and being his messenger are the greatest good in life. From this revelation came his efforts to purify his inner life.

Heal me, O Lord, and I shall be healed, save me, and I shall be saved: for thou art my praise. (17:14)

The popular scholar Albert C. Knudson suggests that the above prayer is the first instance in which the idea of salvation is applied to the inner life alone. The center of gravity of the religious life moved from the outer to the inner world, and the state of the soul became the critical question in religious experience. External ritual gave way to inner awareness. The soul's relationship with the divine was liberated from dependence on outward experience. This is perhaps the profoundest insight from Jeremiah's witness. "He was the human agent through whom the Divine Spirit first revealed the innermost truth and highest form of religious experience."(13)

INSPIRATION

The roots of personal religion can only be perceived when some sense of the *process* of inspiration is rightly understood. The basis of all genuine inspiration is a mind in tune with the infinite, a moral sympathy with the principles on which the universe is governed, and "a consciousness, none the less real because incommunicable, of personal fellowship with the God who reigns over all, and who reveals His secret purpose to His servants the prophets."(14)

The ultimate secret of prophetic inspiration was an immediate consciousness of experiencing the nature of God. Jeremiah is not so much interested in his own person as he is in the fact that he has become a vessel of the divine word, a person in whose individual existence is condensed the relationship between Yahweh and Israel. Though Jeremiah's complaints are deeply personal, they actually transcend the personal. Jeremiah's "I" is the "I" of the people. He identifies himself in moments of inspiration with his people because he bears their contradictions within himself. Of all the prophets, Jeremiah dared to converse with God in a fully human, personal way.

"I WILL WRITE IT UPON THEIR HEARTS"

But this is the covenant which I will make with the house of Israel after those days, says the Lord: "I will put my law within them, and I will write it upon their hearts; and I will be their God, and they shall be my people. (Jeremiah 31:33)

Jeremiah may not have seen that this new relationship to Yahweh must break through the bond of nationalism and be fulfilled in a universal oneness based on experience of God. Yet he announced a New Covenant that was inward and individual, giving to every heart the direct knowledge of its Creator's mercy. The central truth of this new understanding of the divine-human relationship was the inner experience of true religion and the spiritual illumination of the individual mind and conscience.

Twenty-five hundred years have gone by since Jeremiah was inspired to utter the understanding that made him an outcast among his people. Perhaps in our time there are enough receptive souls in whom the seed of new understanding can be planted. Though religious wars continue to plague us, we have learned from the atrocities of inquisitions and crusades of the past. Intolerance is no longer accepted as a sign of spiritual authority. The divine law, that which is required of us for our spiritual evolution, is no longer secret information in the hands of the privileged few. The law remains esoteric only in the sense that it is an *inner* knowledge rather than a hidden knowledge.

Joseph Campbell tells us that one of our problems is that the lines of communication between the conscious and the unconscious have been cut. He writes that "the modern hero-deed must be that of questing to bring to light again the lost Atlantis of the co-ordinated soul."(15)

Campbell observes that the universal triumph of the secular state has thrown all religious organizations into a secondary and impotent position. A transmutation of the whole social order is necessary so that "through every detail and act of secular life the vitalizing image of the universal god-man who is actually immanent and effective in all of us may be somehow made known to consciousness."(16) He concludes that it is necessary for people to understand that the same redemption is revealed through various symbols.

A single song is being inflected through all the colorations of the human choir. General propaganda for one or another of the local solutions, therefore, is superfluous—or much rather, a menace. The way to become human is to learn to recognize the lineaments of God in all of the wonderful modulations of the face of man.(17)

The modern individual cannot wait for his or her community to cast off the "slough of pride, fear, rationalized avarice, and sanctified misunderstanding."(18) We must each find a path that will lead us to a face to face experience with the transforming reality expressed in the religions of all times.

II

The Inner Life and the Institution

THE MODERN SEARCH FOR MEANING

We now live in a time of smorgasbord spirituality, religion *a la carte*, where the lines of authority are blurred and barriers between traditions and cultures are crumbling. These are times of extraordinary possibilities in which humanity's loftiest and most powerful knowledge is being made available to anyone who yearns for it. But therein also lies the danger: confusion and lack of discernment. What is ultimate truth? What is the summit of human transformation?

Religion is meant to awaken us to a life-long process of becoming that is, by definition, nothing less than the blossoming of human beings into children of the universe who live in the light of that sacred mystery which created everything. All spiritual leaders must reflect and transmit something of that light or they are charlatans and impostors. And what is the basic characteristic of this metaphorical light? Unconditional love. To know that we are loved is the secret that religion reveals. It has no other message and no other purpose. But what power that knowledge contains! It is indeed "saving" knowledge. Kierkegaard told us: "If there is an equality among us in which we truly resemble each other, it is that not one of us truly thinks about being loved." It is this "faith," this knowing which gives birth to inner freedom, confident joy, indomitable hope, and radiant love for all other beings. This is what the man from Nazareth came to tell us and it is the very simplicity of his cosmic message that got him nailed to a cross.

Ritual, holy scripture, liturgical celebrations must lead us to this state of consciousness or they are dead ends. Does the straightforward, no-nonsense core of religion mean that we can be rid of temples, fancy robes, musical instruments and all the props that go into creating a religious community? Perhaps, for all of that is only meant to assist the inner experience of awakening to a new consciousness of the divine Presence in our lives. If you can use it, if it works for you, then by all means take advantage of it. Sometimes a chapel or temple is the only place in our society where one can still find silence enabling such an encounter. If, on the other hand, these sets and artifacts reek with negative associations, then walk away from them and find a quiet grove in the woods — if you still can.

The injustices of the world will never be overcome until individuals have changed. And individuals will never change until religion as inner transformation has penetrated to the heart of their being and made them into new persons. Change happens one human being at a time.

It is your transformation, my transformation, that will make a difference in this wondrous but troubled world of ours, as we become who we truly are beyond the mundane limitations of the narrow realities in which we function.

THE ORIGINAL PURPOSE OF THE CHURCH

The word *church* combines several Greek words with a multitude of images and metaphors. It comes directly from a word meaning "those who belong to God." The New Testament writers used many images to express the meaning of church: slaves of Christ, the people of God, the family of God, the bride of Christ, the body of Christ. In the Book of Acts, the term *brothers* is used thirty times to describe the fellowship we call church.

Church is therefore a gathering of individuals who, called together by a stirring in their hearts, seek to awaken to the divine presence. The real building of the church is, in the words of Thomas Merton, "a union of hearts in love, sacrifice, self-transcendence."(1) Merton writes in *Life and Holiness* that "the strength of this building depends on the extent to which the Holy Spirit gains possession of each person's heart, not on the extent to which our exterior conduct is organized and disciplined by an expedient system."(2) Church is simply people who have experienced through the Christ's teachings the truth of Isaiah's prophecy on the coming of *Emmanuel,* God among us, and attempt to make it the center of their lives.

In spite of the chaotic array of religious organizations claiming to be the "real thing," there are only two kinds of churches: the institutional church with its power structure, fund raising, and packaged curriculum; and the holy church which is manifested in the selfless love of individuals both within and outside the organization who have awakened to the reality of the living God.

The churches that surround us today are buildings, operations, projects, bureaucracies. Whether it be the Pope, the elder, the minister who has control over the community, or the families that contribute the most money, the organization is generally run along secular concepts of power and authority. Intolerance, petty rivalry, dogmatic tyranny, group pressure, harsh legalism—the list of perversions is almost endless and stands as a tragic witness to the nearly complete spiritual bankruptcy of the institutional church.

This legacy of degeneration has come to a climax as our society becomes more and more secular and as seekers of spiritual transformation look for other avenues of development. The consciousness of God is very hard to find in Christian worship. Boredom, habit, popular custom, mechanical repetition predominate in what is supposed to be a religious experience. Serious seekers can no longer sit through mediocre sermons that impart nothing, or absurd rituals which pass for the celebration of the intimate presence of the Holy. The church at both the local and national levels is in danger of accepting death and calling it abundant life.

Fundamentalism, that strange throwback to a frontier mentality cut off from all of the illumined teachers of the past, has experienced a surge in membership, a massive return of young people, and rather arrogantly points to this factor as a sign of holding the keys to the truth. This phenomenon is a sad commentary on the desperate need for spiritual food in our time because it forcefully demonstrates that people prefer a place with easy answers over a place that doesn't even know the questions. Emotional stimulation, though far removed from genuine spiritual experience, is better than dreary boredom and mere social interactions posing as Christian *agape*, or conscious love.

The gathered assembly of the faithful ought to be a place where the deeper self awakens and is allowed to arise from beneath the pretenses, masks, defense mechanisms, and ignorance of our superficial selves. For this transformation to occur, the teachings of Christ must penetrate the heart and fill it with a taste of divine love. However, the local church seems to have lost sight of that precious map that leads us toward finding our true selves. The treasury of Christian spiritual writings seems to have been forgotten or rejected, reducing preachers to administrators and social activists while leaving people in the pew in a state of starvation.

THE DEVELOPMENT OF CHRISTIANITY

How could one of the most radical teachings on inner transformation be turned into the foolishness that goes on in most churches on Sunday mornings? The historical reasons began as far back as 312 A.D. when the emperor Constantine won a crucial battle and then decided that his victory was due to the fact that he had experimented with putting crosses on his soldiers' shields. From then on, Christianity became a state religion, as opposed to a secret underground movement that brought certain death to its adherents if they were found out. Now membership was something that could guarantee tax write-offs. Centuries later, the bishop of Rome decided to carve out western Europe for himself and saddled it with a legalistic form of religion that has dominated our societies ever since.

What was lost in the process was the eastern form of Christianity coming out of Palestine, Syria and Egypt. This teaching is truer to the original meaning of the Aramaic expressions spoken by the Christ to Mideastern people. It is more focused on the development of the inner life and has been preserved in the traditions of eastern orthodoxy. In the *Philokalia*, a compilation of sayings of Fathers of the desert, there is a teaching on the watch of the heart and the uses of attention that is as potent a method of human transformation as can be found anywhere.

ORTHODOXY AND GNOSTICISM

One of the clues to the early Christian struggle is found in the conflict between orthodoxy and gnosticism. We know the latter primarily through the polemical writings of its enemies. Vast and complex mythologies that seem to have little value to us are generally associated with gnosticism. However, C. G. Jung's study of the archetypal imagery expressed in these myths has provided some important insights into gnostic thought. But it is more significant to focus on the recognition of the central issues in that struggle because they did shape what was to become official Christianity.

For the first several hundred years of the budding religion, gnostic and orthodox Christians battled for dominance of a world view that came to be known as Christianity. The gnostics and their insistence on the primacy of individual experience lost the power struggle and orthodoxy, with its requirements of obedience to hierarchies and adherence to creeds, took hold of the western soul. Monasticism was tolerated in the organization as a safety valve for those who were driven to the solitary life, but it too was brought under the rule of the group mind represented by the bishop.

THE CONTRIBUTIONS OF GNOSTICISM

For over five decades, Dr. Charles Ashanin studied and taught these matters on several continents. He is professor of Early Church History Emeritus and a practicing Orthodox who is particularly sensitive to the spirit of Christianity.

His rich insights into this struggle are valuable to all seekers of meaning as they exemplify the process by which the teachings are turned into something other than what they were meant to be, sometimes even into their opposite.

Dr. Ashanin suggests that Christianity did not begin as a hierarchical entity, forcing individuals into a group structure. He states that original Christianity was "charismatic" and that although it had a sense of leadership, it was in the context of community rather than *over* community. This "charismatic understanding" included equality within the group. Its leadership was not based on power but on the charisma of those who were advanced either in experience or in knowledge. That situation changed as Christianity became hierarchical.

When the Roman empire became aware of those who followed "the Way" and declared war on them, there evolved a struggle between two societies: the Roman, pagan society with its own religion and this new religion claiming a different kind of theology. These two worlds were at war.

As time went on, hierarchical Christianity adapted the Roman military and bureaucratic structures. A fundamental change occurred when things of the spirit become obedience to the bishop.

Dr. Ashanin points out, however, that these bishops who later became bureaucrats, were called in the early Church *guardian angels* and *pastors*. The hierarchical system was not meant to be authoritarian but was intended to organize a net of support in what was nothing less than a war situation. The hierarchy was not supposed to kill the charismatic spirit but to safeguard it.

Gnosticism was a radical critique of what Christianity was becoming. But it was also an attempt to create Christianity in its own image. It emphasized the spiritual, the egalitarian and real transformation as opposed to the popular version that became a socially accepted institution. The gnostics criticized the leadership of the Church in a way that is still applicable in our day: "Some who do not understand mysteries speak of things which they do not understand but they will boast that the mystery of the truth belongs to them alone."

The gnostics were people who were conscious of the

divine and who saw only bureaucrats in power requiring external deeds to fit the membership of an organization. Dr. Ashanin suggests that within the Church itself, there were sincere people who realized that the Church was bureaucratized. Without denying the theology, doctrines, or symbols of that Church, they went out to live their Christianity separate from the "political" Church. They did not want to live under a regime where bishops were magistrates. The whole movement of monasticism came as a corrective. The criticism of the gnostics had a positive impact on this segment of the Church which disassociated itself politically but remained spiritually within it as a guardian of the spiritual dimension.

Yet it remains possible that the Church left out key insights into the message of Christ by choosing specific gospels over others during the political struggle dealing with the books officially included in the Bible. Other gnostic insights that were lost in this process include those regarding the intriguing role of Mary Magdalene. The gnostics claimed that she, rather than Peter, was the primary apostle and thereby included that whole feminine dimension that has been missing from Christianity for centuries.

Gnostic Christians insisted that baptism did not make a Christian and in the *Gospel of Philip* it is written that "many people go down into the water and come up without having received anything and claim to be Christians."

In the legalistic Church, the act itself makes something valid. But Dr. Ashanin points out that the gnostic criticism of external ritual is unfair. It is true that in our time, many churches seem to adhere to the unfortunate motto: "you all come, so long as you pray, pay, and obey." But in the early Church, a long process was required for becoming a Christian. Christianity was once an initiation into a mystery, into an inward truth rather than into some external fact. The Church had its own gnostic initiation which generated an inner understanding of the Christian mysteries.

Dr. Ashanin concludes that without the Church which gnostics opposed, there would not have been gnosticism as we know it. Without gnosticism, the theological outlook of the Church would not have been the same. Gnosticism forced the Church to intellectualize Christian thought at the expense of its spiritual side in order to define its truth against so-called heresies. Yet becoming a true *pneumatikoi* (spiritual one) ought to remain the vocation of every Christian.

CHRISTIANITY IN OUR TIME

The mystics of the fourteenth century, the era of Renaissance, and the events of the Reformation certainly resisted the more grotesque distortions imposed on the Churches, such as the sale of indulgences. But by the time we reach the American frontier of the nineteenth century, we find a new misinterpretation unexpectedly born out of these attempts at purification. Biblical literalism, the basis of fundamentalism, was made possible because the "baby was thrown out with the bath water." The effort of *restoration* (returning Christianity to its original New Testament expression) combined with a general ignorance of the great teachers of the faith to create a dangerous mutation of the teachings. By dropping all the wisdom developed through the centuries, from Clement of Alexandria in the second century to Meister Eckhart in the fourteenth, the preachers traveling through the new territories often turned the Scriptures into a one dimensional caricature, thereby overlooking the clear injunction that "the letter kills, but the spirit gives life." Gone was the allegorical method of Origen and Augustine (interpreting the scriptures as symbol and metaphor for inward spiritual truth), gone was the poetic intuitive understanding of John of the Cross or of Ephrem the Syrian. Suddenly, a new phenomenon was on the religious scene: bibliolatry. Stripped of its bottomless spiritual depths informed by Hebrew mysticism and a consciousness of the universal Logos, the Bible now became a weapon of separation rather than a roadmap to unity.

This misuse of sacred writings was countered by the "historical critical method" which still reigns in seminaries to this day. Here the findings of archeology along with the application of rational and secular forms of literary criticism are the foundation for the exegesis of Biblical texts. Though identifying the context in which a teaching was given is certainly superior to a dull acceptance of every jot and tiddle as the divine expression, we are still left with the same gaping black hole. What is the inner meaning of the teachings that has the power to transform human beings? The inability to answer this question is the source of the modern churches' irrelevance to the spiritual journey.

The god of most religious organizations is not the "cosmic Christ" but the rational mind. The leadership, still predominantly male and over fifty, stands squarely before the gates of the kingdom of heaven like the Pharisees of old. They are the ones of whom Christ said: "Woe to you, scribes and Pharisees, hypocrites! Because you shut the kingdom of heaven against men; for you neither enter yourselves nor allow those who would enter to go in." (Matthew 23:13) Their justification for avoiding the true demands of Christ ("you must be reborn"), is found in nice catch-phrases like "peace and justice." We would all agree that the world needs plenty of those, but the person without inner peace is not going to spread peace in the outer world! It is much easier to decry the Third World debt and to lobby in the halls of Congress than it is to overcome one's negativity, self-indulgence and egotism.

For generations, the church as we know it has reinforced our culture and often blatantly stood for the opposite of its teaching. Merely the small detail of a flag in the sanctuary invalidates the church's claim to be the house of God. Nationalism does not mix with a consciousness of the universal love that unites all things.

THE POTENTIAL OF THE CHRISTIAN WAY

Why is it that persons who have journeyed through esoteric and new age teachings or who have left the Church altogether sometimes find themselves returning to this anachronism in what is essentially a post-Christian society? The fact is that we have no choice but to deal with Christianity in some way. Most of us born and bred in western culture carry in our subconscious the values of the

Judeo-Christian tradition. We have been molded by these ideas, as has our society and our history. We cannot stamp them out any more than we can choose not to be born from the parents life has given us. A number of the great spiritual teachers of our day have commented on this, including G. I. Gurdjieff and Karlfried Graf Dürckheim, suggesting that our essence is formed by our cultural heritage and it is in this context that we can best develop the inner life.

In other words, though there is much to learn from Hindu and Buddhist insights, westerners may find that their "native soil" is best suited for the teachings of Jesus of Nazareth. For instance, we will tend to naturally resonate with the idea that every person can be an incarnation, or at least an instrument of the divine, whereas the concept of becoming one with the great Void is not as likely to have the meaning it does for a child who has grown up in the shadow of the Buddha in meditation.

It is also true that the institutional religion has been unable to destroy the treasure buried within its dogmas. Perhaps its purpose through history has been to unknowingly carry this spiritual wealth hidden beneath its wretched robes of patriarchy, bureaucracy, greed and ignorance so that genuine seekers of truth might have access to these living waters.

One clue that points to the presence of life beneath the rubble of nonsense and distortion making up the contemporary church is found in the list of rather extraordinary individuals who have incarnated this treasure in the concrete actions of their daily lives. Consider this roster in our century alone: Albert Schweitzer, Nicolas Berdayev, Evelyn Underhill, Thomas Merton, C.S. Lewis, Mother Teresa, Alexander Solzhenitsyn, Malcolm Muggeridge. There are many others, of course, famous and unknown who bear witness to the incredible transformation available through the teaching preserved in the church. These are people whose inner life caught fire and metamorphosized them into radiant children of the divine Spirit. Their impact on the world around them is undeniable and the illumination within their being is as wondrous as any esoteric mystery.

Each of these people discovered that the dogmas so poorly preached from the pulpits are carriers of experiential wisdom. They developed "ears to hear and eyes to see" in spite of all the obstacles, particularly that of the church itself. The outer form of this teaching, which knows nothing of its inner content, will continue to attract persons satisfied with simple ritual and friendly Sunday morning fellowship. Yet the Church will also continue to attract people yearning for deeper meaning and new becoming. If they do not abandon the effort in despair or disgust, they will be the ones to call the church to its authentic task. They will rediscover the revelations of Christ and the way that leads to a commingling with the divine. They will be the ones to find the genuine spiritual leaders, the few enlightened pastors who have not been destroyed by seminaries addicted to academia, and together they will create a new community aligned with the legacy of early Christianity.

There are such places on this planet. I have found one in eastern France, and I am privileged to count among my friends a number of individuals who have made it through the trackless waste of external religion to the well of spiritual transformation. Every generation has produced such persons and they pass on the torch in the dark night of human ignorance. This is why those who seek spiritual awakening cannot entirely disregard the Church in spite of itself. It is a vessel that carries a sacred cargo, one that is known to give life to those who find it. And the most astonishing thing of all is that this secret cargo often draws the seeker to itself long before he or she has any idea that it exists.

The paradox, then, remains virtually irresolvable: Does the Church as we find it in our time foster the inner life? No. Does the Church hold the keys to a new consciousness? Yes. In the last few years, signs of hope have appeared concerning the Church's role in the future. The influx into ministry of women and of persons who have journeyed through the holistic mindset of the new age promises to impact the Church's teachings. Also, the resurgence of eastern Christianity in the west is providing us with a theology steeped in insights that are both highly pragmatic and profoundly mystical, although they are not any more generally accessible in mainstream Orthodoxy than they are in Protestant or Catholic churches.

Furthermore, those who are on the spiritual journey need to look beyond the cobwebs of old associations that hang over the teachings of Christ. Rejecting the external trappings of a religion that seems like rotted fruit about to fall from the tree of civilization does not imply rejecting the experience to which it originally called us: the transmutation of human consciousness through the indwelling of divine light. The great visionary mystics of Christianity, many of whom were persecuted by their *mother,* the Church, offer powerful testimony to the worthiness of the teaching. Whether or not the vessel that carries this cargo is doomed to crash upon the rocks of its own failures is of little concern. The real issue is: can a new community of enlightened persons, radiantly humble and intimate with the divine—the true mark of lovers of God—arise out of the ashes?

THE VESSEL'S SACRED CARGO

What then is this cargo so well concealed from both its gatekeepers and those who "hunger and thirst after righteousness?" This cargo has become known at different times in history. The teachings have been clothed in the expression of different cultures but their results are essentially the same: the creation of individuals who have so transcended their egos that they have become transparent to the unconditional love sustaining the universe.

Religion here reveals its true purpose. It reconnects us with our origin, lifting us out of the mundane illusions in which we swim daily, rendering us conscious of the invisible but dynamic presence of something completely *other* and yet incredibly familiar.

Christ spoke of becoming as little children in order to enter the consciousness he named "the kingdom of heaven." This is a universal truth echoed in the teaching of Socrates: wonder. Religion is meant to reawaken our awareness of the sacred nature of reality. It heals us from the numbing apathy , we so often feel toward the little things of life.

Religion centers us not on ourselves but on this mystery called *God* that actively seeks to bring us face to face with its Presence. It offers methods of transformation that have been tested by time and by some of the great souls of humanity. These are priceless teachings that are available to all who yearn to become who they truly are and to penetrate into the ultimate secrets of existence.

The Church contains the repository of potent inner disciplines that structure the inner spiritual combat and lead to ineffable discoveries. The Scriptures refer to these stages of new becoming with terms like "cleansing the cup," "new wine," and the famous *metanoia* so poorly translated as "repent" but which suggests rather a metamorphosis of the mind where repentance is only a stage. Detailed systems of inner development can be found in the Church, from the methods on discernment of the fourth century Church father Evagarius to Ignatius of Loyola on active meditation, and Orthodoxy's spiritual giant Symeon the New Theologian on encountering the divine light. Highly charged words like recollection, contemplation, centering, vigilance, surrender, and remembrance run parallel to the more familiar Christian ideas such as forgiveness, love, and humility that are found in Scripture. This latter concept, so central to this path of enlightenment, has perhaps been the most misrepresented insight of all. Humility is the absence of vanity and self-interest; it is the recognition of our true condition, and the only state of being through which we can properly receive

God. In his book *Living Presence*, Kabir Helminsky defines humility as the awareness of our dependence on the One. This state does not refer to resignation or to the "meek and mild" image of Christ that so disgusted William Blake. The young rabbi from the rugged hillsides of Galilee was anything but such a person. And he certainly did not intend to have his message turned into a "let's be good boys and girls" sermon typical of so many middle class churches. On the contrary, he warned us that his teaching is as sharp and divisive as a sword, that it would in fact cause a great deal of trouble to those who took it seriously.

The teachings contained in the vaults and libraries of the Church offer insights into every nuance of inner transformation. This understanding comes out of the furnace of experience and is grounded in the flesh and blood of the lovers of God who have gone before us. Here is the true legacy of the Church and the purpose of the religious community. Out of the wealth of its inheritance and the inspiration of dedicated and enlightened leaders, the Church could be the doorway to extraordinary possibilities for the individual and for our society. Religion could once again claim its role as transforming experience rather than remaining the caretaker of rigid and irrelevant dogma.

The latest Gallup polls tell us that over ninety-five percent of Americans believe in God or a universal spirit, but only forty percent are part of a church community. Imagine what would happen in the local sanctuary if that other fifty-five percent showed up looking to be nourished by the "living bread." That is how the reformation started, with lay movements simply creating their own communities since the clergy was unable to provide them with what they truly needed. These groups shared in common a burning need for transformation. Out of their gathering came some of the greatest masterpieces of spiritual literature, such as *The Imitation of Christ* by Thomas a Kempis, *The Theologia Germanica* written by the Friends of God under the tutelage of Meister Eckhart and *The Spiritual Combat* by Lorenzo Scupoli (later enhanced by Theophan the Recluse and retitled *Unseen Warfare*). Those fires have since burned out and the wells of living waters they uncovered have dried up. History has come full circle. It is time for a new reformation and this implies a return to religion's first love: encounter with the sacred.

The next section will present the essence of Christian teaching through the prism of its transforming impact on the individual. We are therefore moving from the outer expression to the inner meaning of this religion. This process is critical to all traditions as their truth, power and oneness can only be found through the spiritual awakening they generate. Our purpose here will be to reflect upon certain key insights of Christian teachings that provide a universal compass for applying their wisdom.

III

The Journey Inward

INNER MEANINGS

In exploring the inner meaning of spiritual teachings, it is necessary to go beyond the standard dogmas that are passed on through catechism, Sunday-school classes and theological seminaries. From the very beginning, there was an inner understanding of the teachings that had to be uncovered. Jesus said to his disciples: "To you has been given the secret of the kingdom of God, but for those outside everything is in parables." (Mark 4:11) Contemporary theologians are very uncomfortable with this and they try to dismiss it along with other sayings such as "the Kingdom of God is within you" which is consistently translated "among you" because they cannot accept the implications of that little Greek preposition *en*.

But these are issues for scholastic minds lost in abstraction and afraid to enter the darkness of their own inner worlds. For people of the so-called *baby boom generation*, the awareness of other states of consciousness was never a serious problem. I entered upon my search for spiritual awakening in the mid-1970's, at a time when drugs and offbeat metaphysical literature were prime roadmaps for those who sought contact with greater meaning. In that decade, there were people loose in American society who had encountered such radical experiences, especially in the jungles of Viet Nam, that all shreds of mainstream thinking and behavior had gone by the wayside.

SEEKING IN THE DARKNESS

Out of what seemed like sheer coincidence, a book was lent to me by a friend at a time of particular need. It was a historical study of an ancient brotherhood of secret initiates who were brought into a rare enlightenment in an age of great darkness. This was no plot for a second rate movie, but the lived experience of seekers from another era. I was especially struck by the fact that they were seeking for the same thing: a transformation of self into a consciousness of the deep mysteries of the human spirit and its cosmic origin. This new life is the same in all centuries, in all cultures, in all religions: it is the Higher Self, the death of the little, invented, fragmented self; it is oneness, wholeness.

I soon began reading book after book: Eastern philosophy, esoteric teachings, scientific studies on human consciousness. The more I searched, the more I became certain that something was guiding me. The right book would fall into my hands at the right time. These books were food for my soul, creating a new life within, leading me onward toward a goal I knew nothing about, though I was beginning to realize in some mysterious way that there was something very great to be found.

One thing is certain: any search for transforming Truth,

the kind that opens the inner sight to a radically new sense of reality, cannot be undertaken on the surface of society. That plane is made up exclusively of the search for food, mates, and success. It is the world of the absurd where people seem to be born in order to pay the rent, produce more consumers and workers for the anthill, and then die when their value as laborers is over. In such a life, there is no mystery, no wonder, no higher purpose, no hope.

Those who intuitively recognize that this cannot possibly be the sum total of the purpose for existence must find their way into deeper undercurrents of civilization where another kind of knowledge is available to humanity, beyond the "eat or be eaten" syndrome. Unfortunately, these subterranean levels include all sorts of quicksand, and one must be prepared to struggle with dangerous traps in order to reach higher planes of understanding.

I found myself drawn into a bizarre world that lay on the outskirts of the search for deeper knowledge. It was the world of psychics and astrologers, tarot card readers and healers. I came across individuals who lived with one foot in previous lives, or at least a foot in something other than what passes for reality. They fascinated me at first, for they had found a way to color their otherwise dull, ordinary lives with the most outlandish fantasies. These persons live in a permanent fog separating them from the more mundane reality of things like grocery shopping. To believe that you were once an heir to the throne in medieval Scotland is like taking a potent injection of self-importance while the world around you writes you off as just a common individual.

I was soon moving along the periphery of the community of psychics and spiritualists that has captivated the human mind from the dawn of civilization. This blind hunger for experience of a wiser, vaster plane of reality comes from a deep inner yearning. It is particularly prevalent now that the worldview of the dominant cultures excludes this reality. Quite often, this need for experience of the transcendent is distorted into a return to the ancient world of omens and amulets, curses and visitations, which seems more interesting than the world of shopping malls and fast food restaurants.

My acquaintances indiscriminately gathered together all the eccentric characters of history, from Nostradamus to Count Saint-Germain and Madame Blavatsky, threw in as many secret societies as they could come up with, mixed it all together and created an elixir of fantasy that gave them weird dreams and a reason to get up in the morning. The trouble was that they had their hands on half-truths that attracted naive seekers who could not find signposts to spiritual reality in the world of Wall Street, the evening news, and home computers. Anyone with a taste for the invisible aspects of existence can hardly help being intrigued by the occult mysteries. I hoped that beneath all the mumbo-jumbo was a genuine desire to overcome our petty, self-centered level of awareness in order to encounter the holy. But I soon realized that these people were wandering in the fog of their over-stimulated imaginations.

One odd little man once assured me that he was one of the hundred and forty-four thousand souls mentioned in the

Book of Revelation who would survive the nuclear holocaust foreseen by some visionary, and would find himself beamed up to a space ship described in the teachings of Hermes. That one was too hard to swallow even for a gullible young man whose search for the unknown urged him forward without a compass. But then I met an old blind woman sitting behind a curtain in a darkened church who held my watch in her hand, concentrated on the energies it had absorbed from constant contact with my wrist, and told me that I would be taking a trip to Asia. Here I was, penniless, unemployed, without even the means to get to the nearest drugstore, and being told by a stranger that such a voyage would take place within a few months. The woman's simplicity, kindness, and down-home honesty kept me from classifying her as one more fraud along the way. And two months later, from completely out of the blue, I found myself sitting in an airplane on a thirty-two hour flight to Bangkok! Facts are hard to argue with. The trip was meant to take my mind off of astrological charts and mystic writings. However, the land of wandering monks, ever-present incense at roadside shrines, and underground temples dating back hundreds of years, was hardly the place to convince me that returning to the rat-race of a greed-driven society was the way to live. It was under the pastel colors of the Asian sky that I experienced the transcendental dimensions of meditation.

The very rhythm of life was conducive to quiet reflection. The exotic surroundings and ancient monuments confirmed that what I sought could be found. Human transformation was not simply a hot selling topic in *New Age* bookstores. It had been going on for centuries throughout the world and particularly in this Buddhist setting caressed by the gentle winds of the South China Sea.

In this brief interlude from the noise and madness of Western civilization, among elephants and monkeys, painted gods and peaceful shrines, I decided to devote my life to the search that had begun haphazardly in the haze of inner longing and alienation. The geography of the East materialized for me a new awareness of how different life could be from the hustle and bustle of the big cities I had frequented back home. I no longer had to rely on my imagination to invent some mythic world where higher consciousness was possible. Planet Earth is the stage where this evolution is meant to occur.

Back in the United States, I returned to my somewhat bohemian lifestyle. I knew something was around the corner, something that would change the course of my life. I was now ready to sacrifice everything, even my childhood dreams, in order to receive the enlightenment that alone could show me the purpose of life and the way to fulfill my contribution to the universe.

I was to discover the great irony that the very thing I ran away from—the Christian teachings—contained more mystery and wonder than anything I had experienced in my exotic wanderings.

THE INDWELLING OF THE UNCREATED

The ancient Scriptures that are the foundation of Christianity invite us to seek after the mystery and power that we name God. They tell us that this unknown and yet very present creative force of the universe responds to us individually. But they add that a personal contact must be established to enable our participation in this new consciousness.

Such a divine-human relationship is often expressed by the New Testament writers in terms of indwelling:

"You in me, and I in you." (John 14:20)

"The Kingdom of Heaven is within you." (Luke 17:21)

"You know him (the Spirit), for he dwells with you, and will be in you." (John 14:17)

"It is no longer I who live, but Christ who lives in me." (Galatians 2:20)

These words express the indescribable intimacy possible between human beings and that dimension of reality we call *the Divine*. The experience of this encounter yields a transformation, a becoming which is the entrance into another dimension of reality known in the symbolism of religious language as *life eternal*. "And this is eternal life, that they know the only true God, and Jesus Christ whom thou hast sent" (John 17:3).

This highest state of consciousness that Paul called "the peace that passes all understanding" has been given many names.

At the turn of the century, R.M. Bucke called it "cosmic consciousness." Zen Buddhism names it *Satori*, in Yoga it is *Samadhi*, in Taoism they know it as "the absolute Tao."

In our day, Thomas Merton used the phrase

"transcendental unconscious" while Abraham Maslow describes it as "peak experience"; the Sufis speak of *Fana* and G.I. Gurdjieff labeled it "objective consciousness" while the Quakers experience it as "the Inner Light." Karlfried Graf Dürckheim calls it the "breakthrough of Being."

What is meant by these mysterious expressions of experience—enlightenment, illumination, liberation, mystical oneness? At its most basic level, we are dealing with a state of awareness that is radically different from our ordinary understanding. The word *mysticism*, so abused and rejected in mainstream religious circles, simply suggests an expansion of consciousness beyond the ordinary boundaries of our egos to a state where union with a greater reality is achievable.

THE MYSTICS

Evelyn Underhill defines mysticism as "the hunger for reality, the unwillingness to be satisfied with the purely animal or the purely social level of consciousness."(1) This is the first and essential stage in the development of a mystical consciousness.

In attempting a definition, it is perhaps more important to consider what mysticism involves rather than what it is.

Briefly stated, mysticism calls for a relentless effort in the concentration of thought, will and love upon the eternal realities that are commonly ignored. An attitude of attention, best described as a state of prayer, is required.

The readjustments which shall make this attention natural and habitual are a phase in man's inward conflict for the redemption of consciousness from its lower and partial attachments. The downward drag is incessant, and can be combated only by those who are clearly aware of it, and are willing to sacrifice lower interests and joys to the demands of the spiritual life.(2)

The mystic way is therefore a process of sublimation carrying the relationship of the self with the universe to higher levels than our ordinary states of awareness. But this is no selfish journey. For as the mystic grows nearer the source of true life and participates in the creative energies of the Divine, he or she is capable of greater unselfish activity. Among the mystics in the Christian tradition are found missionaries, preachers, prophets, social reformers, poets, founders of institutions, servants of the poor and the sick, and instructors of the soul.

The mystic is not merely a self going out on a solitary quest of Reality. He can, and must, and does go only as a member of the whole body, performing as it were the function of a specialized organ. What he does, he does for all.(3)

Evelyn Underhill points to three ways in which the mystical consciousness comes through humanity:

1. The apostolic type: people of action, dynamic manifestations of the Spirit.

2. The prophetic type: people of supreme vision, who enlarge the horizons of the world.

3. The martyr-type: people of utter sacrifice and complete interior surrender.

These three types show us the way out of our spiritual

shortcomings and lead us toward reconciliation with God. Their devotional lives reveal to us the most direct way to an attainment of the consciousness of the Presence of God.

We learn from the writings of the mystics that such a consciousness has the power to lift those who possess it to a plane of reality that no struggle, no cruelty, no catastrophe can disturb. This "inner sanctuary" is the point where God and the soul touch. In the fourteenth century, John Tauler referred to this place as "the ground of the soul." Catherine of Siena spoke of the "interior home of the heart," Teresa of Avila knew it as the "inner castle," and John of the Cross described it as the "house at rest in darkness and concealment." These metaphors suggest a secret dwelling in the center of our being that remains permanently united with God's creative act. The self in its deepest nature is more than itself. To move into oneself means ultimately to move beyond oneself. But this does not wrap us in a selfish isolation from the pain and responsibility of life. Rather, it renews and empowers us to reach out to others in truly meaningful ways. Evelyn Underhill tells us that such inner transformation helps the mystics to enter, more completely than ever before, into the life of the group to which they belong.

> It will teach them to see the world in a truer proportion, discerning eternal beauty beyond and beneath apparent ruthlessness. It will educate them in a charity free from all taint of sentimentalism; it will confer on them an unconquerable hope.(4)

Out of her vast study and personal experience, Underhill

offers us one of the finest definitions of *mysticism*: "Mysticism is the way of union with Reality. The mystic is a person who has attained that union in greater or lesser degree; or who aims at and believes in such attainment." (5) The history of the Christian religion cannot be separated from the history of its mystics, for the doctrines represent their experiences translated into dogma. The Church's teachings concerning new birth, divine sonship, regeneration, union with Christ are all of mystical origin in that they are derived from concrete experiences rather than from speculation. Such experiences are not the exclusive possession of spiritually sensitive persons. In the state of humble receptivity, the human spirit can apprehend a reality greater than itself.

There is today a great renewal of interest in the cultivation of the spiritual life. Yet churches are emptying like broken cisterns while thousands of seekers are turning toward teachings that provide pragmatic means to generate real change. One of the teachers to have greatly impacted the spiritual evolution of the West in our century is George Ivanovich Gurdjieff (died 1949) whose teachings are presented in chapter seven. He points to the heart of the problem:

> Christianity says precisely this, to love all men. But this is impossible. At the same time it is true that it is necessary to love. First one must be able, only then can one love. Unfortunately, with time, modern Christians have adopted the second half, to love, and lost view of the first, the religion which should have preceded it.(6)

Throughout Western history, the Church has

emphasized the goal of human life and underplayed or neglected the means by which this goal may be reached. The result has been a certain recognizable personality and behavior that is imitated and not the outcome of real inner transformation. Jacob Needleman, a major contributor to the modern spiritual journey, asks the following question in his study of Christianity: what is the bridge that can lead a person from the state of submersion in egoistic emotions to that incomparable range of life known under the simple term "love of God"? In attempting to penetrate to the heart of religious teachings, we must first understand certain key ideas. They establish both our relationship to the teachings and the inner conditions through which we appropriate them.

FAITH AND BELIEF

We are part of a culture in which religion is mostly a matter of words, exhortations, and philosophy, rather than practical guidance for experiencing directly the truth of the teachings. Methods and exercises, such as are found in the writings of the early Fathers of the desert contained in *The Philokalia*, once brought the possibility of growing beyond our ordinary self-centered psychology. But our age has cast them aside in its disdain for anything that cannot be entirely comprehended by the rational mind. Because of this prejudice, the sacred response of faith that emanates from a higher level within us than the ego in search of dominance and comfort has become confused with a kind of *belief* that Needleman calls "one of the numerous egotistic mechanisms within the mind that seem designed solely for the purpose of making people feel they are in the right and that everything is going to be all right."(7)

Maurice Nicoll, whose striking insight into interpreting religious teaching will be discussed in chapter five, presents us with an utterly different understanding of faith. "Faith is a continual inner effort, a continual altering of the mind, of the habitual ways of thought, of the habitual ways of taking everything, of habitual reactions. To act from faith is to act beyond the range of the ideas and reasons that the sense-known side of the world has built up in everyone's mind."(8)

The dichotomy between knowing and believing rests on the fact that what the intellect knows may contradict what the heart believes. Christianity has always recognized that *thinking* by itself cannot bring about a change in human nature. Christ's teachings do not merely offer an explanation of life but rather a means of making life different. It is obvious to everyone that, while we may think great thoughts, we may not be able to live according to what we know to be true. As long as our emotional life remains the same, full of self-justification and negativity, all the right thinking in the world will not change our essential nature. It is not that the mind cannot form a thought of God, but that such thoughts in themselves cannot change anything in us. Something else is required. Tradition tells us that there is within us a force that draws us toward Truth, and this force is neither the thinking function nor the emotional function. This is what the word *faith* is meant to stand for, but it cannot be equated with belief in the sense of a conviction of the emotions opposed to intellectual explanations.

Thomas Merton tells us that faith is neither an emotion nor an opinion. "It is not some personal myth of your own that you cannot share with anyone else, and the objective validity of which does not matter either to you or God or anybody else."(9) For Merton, faith does not bypass the mind, but perfects it. "It puts the intellect in possession of Truth which reason cannot grasp by itself."(10)

The act of faith is also a contact, a communion of wills. Merton observed that, in the *state* of faith, we experience the presence of God. "Faith is the opening of an inward eye, the eyes of the heart, to be filled with the presence of the Divine light."(11)

Something must be awakened in us that is both highly individual, the holistic blossoming of our true self, and at the same time free from mere subjectivity; something both intensely our own yet free of the ego's tyranny.

THE EGO

The ego is defined by Merton as a self-constructed illusion that has our body and part of our soul at its disposal because it has taken over the functions of the inner self. We are turned inside out so that the ego plays the part of the whole person. But the ego is the outer self, that part of us that is going to disappear into nothingness. This is the reason that, in all authentic religious traditions, the way to reality is the way of humility because humility causes us to reject the invented self and accept the *empty* self. Gurdjieff pointed out that one of our most critical mistakes is the illusion concerning our sense of unity. We are not merely one person, but "legions."

> His 'I' changes as quickly as his thoughts, feelings, and moods, and he makes the profound mistake in considering himself always one and the same person; in reality he is always a different person, not the one he was a moment ago.(12)

Our every thought and desire has a life separate and independent from the whole. With a little neutral self-observation, we will notice that we are made of thousands of separate I's, often unknown to each other. The changes in I's is controlled by accidental influences. The sight of a plate of food stimulates a hungry I; a snide remark from a colleague calls forth an angry, self-righteous I. There is nothing in us able to control the change of I's, mainly because we do not notice this phenomenon. Each separate I acts in the name of the whole person. This explains why people so often make decisions and so seldom carry them out. We generally respond to the events acting on us from the outside world. Occasionally we are less caught up in what we are doing and become aware of our existence in the here and now. But it is always a fleeting experience and life soon swallows us again and we slip back into unawareness. Religious teachings are meant to lead us away from the noisy regions of our minds toward the more silent areas of consciousness. This necessitates a control over our thoughts. But this is a difficult path to tread because our attention is always being caught by the ceaseless chattering in our heads. Yet there are witnesses in all centuries who testify to the fact that it is possible to reach a state of pure consciousness without thought, a state in which truth is revealed to us directly without the use of words. This is the encounter with the sacred.

THE SOUL

One of the great errors of the Christian tradition may be that the presence of a soul already formed and functioning was taken for granted. Yet the soul is not a fixed entity but an actual energy that is activated in the experiences of daily life. The assumption of a soul in finished form within human nature has led to identifying our ordinary thoughts and emotions with the higher part of ourselves, and thus to the mistaken effort of trying to perfect our being by perfecting our thoughts and emotions. But our spiritual growth does not come through merely intellectual or emotional development. There is another state of being to be reached, another quality of awareness that reveals to us new aspects of reality.

According to Father Silouan, an Orthodox monk of Mount Athos—the island off the coast of Greece that has been home to men of prayer for a thousand years—the Christian teachings tell us that our psychological functions are incapable of altering themselves. Change and transformation can come only through the action of an objectively higher force—the Spirit acting upon the soul.

Our job, then, is to become an open cup, sensitive to the movements of the Spirit and prepared to respond to its inspiration. In our day, there is perhaps no more difficult effort. We are blinded by a drive for ceaseless motion, for a constant sense of achievement, for visible results, and we believe that we can only please God by doing a dozen things at once. In line with all the great teachers of spirituality, Thomas Merton argued that the secret of inner peace is detachment. "You will never be able to have perfect interior peace and recollection unless you are detached even from the desire of peace and recollection."(13)

RECOLLECTION

All religious traditions call us to a change of spiritual focus and an attuning of the whole soul to what is beyond and above ourselves. It is a turning of our being toward spiritual things. As spiritual things are simple, recollection is a simplification of our state of mind which gives us the kind of peace and vision that Jesus spoke of when he said: "if your eye is sound, your whole body will be full of light" (Matthew 6:22). Recollection is more than a mere turning inward upon ourselves, and it does not necessarily mean the denial of external things. Recollection makes us aware of what is most significant in the moment of time in which we are living. When the outward self is submissive and ordered by the inward being, then the soul is in harmony with itself, with the realities around it, and with God. When we are not present to ourselves through recollection, then we are only aware of that mode of our being that turns outward to created things. We then lose ourselves in them. Recollection aligns the outward self with the inward self and gives us access to the Spirit. An example of this condition is given to us by the German psychotherapist and spiritual teacher, Karlfried Graf

Dürckheim, whose insight is presented in chapter seven. He tells us that the simple act of watering a flower can be done merely because the plant needs water. But it can also be undertaken as an act of love. The moment is then transformed from an ordinary activity forgotten as quickly as it occurs into a profound and memorable experience that introduces us into the presence of spiritual reality both within ourselves and in the material world.

CONTEMPLATION

The scientist Robert Ornstein has suggested that biofeedback holds great promise for spiritual evolution. Feedback enables a person to hold his or her physiological state constant for a long period of time, which in turn may enable a mode of operation of the nervous system that can be monitored and correlated with other measures of consciousness. According to Ornstein, this type of research might allow us to develop an external index of inner states of consciousness so that experimenters may be able to stimulate the desired nervous system conditions. The alpha rhythm identified in biofeedback indicates a diminution of information-processing activity in a given area of the brain. Alpha waves, particularly during meditation, are generally enhanced. Ornstein noticed that the higher mammals can be regarded as machines that are capable of "retuning" themselves in accordance with alterations in their external environment.(14) This selectivity and tuning can be seen in a place where several people are talking at the same time. We can listen to one person speaking and then tune them out and listen to another person. We therefore continually tune ourselves to suit our needs and expectations, though we are usually not aware of this. When we are hungry, we see more restaurants. When after a meal our need for food has diminished, so does the attractiveness of food in general. We are able to reprogram and reconstruct our awareness based on our motivation. Higher states of consciousness include an awareness that allows every stimulus to enter into the field of our consciousness without the filtering action from our normal selection process. This state of awareness is often pictured in various traditions as a mirror. In Zen Buddhism it is said that the perfected person employs his or her mind as a mirror in that it grasps nothing and refuses nothing. Certain religious traditions also claim that it is possible to perceive the world directly without interference from our personal psychological processes. Ornstein suggests that this state can be thought of as a diminution of the interactive nature of awareness, a state in which we do not select, nor associate to past experience, but in which all possible categories are held in awareness at once. What the Chinese might describe as a gentle standing out of the way or an emptying of the mind, we in the West might see as a violent death of the ego. But this self-sacrifice, which is a sacrifice of vanity and illusion, is the entryway into another consciousness of who we are. This new landscape is uncovered in the effort of contemplation.

Contemplation is precisely the awareness that this *I* is really *not I* and the awakening of the unknown *I* that is beyond observation and reflection and is incapable of commenting upon itself.(15)

Nothing could be more alien to contemplation than the "I think therefore I am" of Descartes. This is the declaration of an alienated person, in "exile from his own spiritual depths."(16) Merton believed that if a person's thought is necessary as a medium through which he or she arrives at the concept of his existence, "then he is in fact only moving further away from his true being."(17) By reducing ourselves to a concept, it becomes impossible for us to experience directly the mystery of our own being. Contemplation does not arrive at reality after a process of deduction, but by an intuitive awakening in which our personal reality becomes fully alive to its own depths.

Above all, contemplation does not result from our choosing to wake ourselves, but from God who chooses to awaken us. Merton asserts that through this experience we come to know and love God in God's very essence and that this is the reason for our creation. Compared with the pure comprehension of love in which we are permitted to see the truth not so much by seeing it as by being absorbed into it, our ordinary ways of seeing and knowing are little more than blindness. Then we may cry out in wonder with the Apostle: "O the depths of the riches of the wisdom and knowledge of God!" Out of his own profound spiritual experience, Thomas Merton shares with us an extraordinary expression of the state of contemplation:

> All variety, all complexity, all paradox, all multiplicity cease . . . Nothing more is desired. A supernatural instinct teaches us that the function of this abyss of freedom that has opened out within our own midst is

to draw us utterly out of our own selfhood and into its immensity of liberty and joy . . . You feel as though you were at last fully born. All that went before was a mistake, a fumbling preparation for birth. And yet now you have become nothing. You have sunk to the center of your own poverty, and there you have felt the doors fly open into infinite freedom, into a wealth which is perfect because none of it is yours and yet it all belongs to you . . . These depths, they are love. And in the midst of you they form a wide, impregnable country.(18)

The forces of energy involved at the heart of the process require a receptivity and vividness that are not part of our ordinary state of awareness. Meister Eckhart, one of the giants of Christian mysticism, counseled that we should be like people always on watch. "The man to whom God is ever present, and who controls and uses his mind to the highest degree, that man alone knows what peace is and he has the Kingdom of Heaven within him."(19)

Jacob Needleman and others who are discovering new means of spiritual growth suggest that the manifestation of love as expressed in religious teaching is possible only to the degree that a person has transmitted the truth to the whole of himself or herself. This requires some kind of *self-mastery* and unrelenting commitment. Methods for this kind of inner effort are presented in Part Two.

When we speak of detachment, contemplation, sanctification, we are seeking to express a phenomenon that affects every part of our organism. The current research in biological and psychological laboratories gives us empirical evidence of actual occurrences that verify the teachings of the major religions. The anthropologist Roger Westcott, for instance, offers the hypothesis that consciousness is endocrinal bioluminescence, suggesting that awareness may consist of the internal generation and reception of perceptible radiation, of a form of light generated in, by, and for the brain.(20)

We need powerful and practical tools to become receptive to this light. We live in an age when the teaching must be rediscovered in ourselves, for only then will it have the power to renew our lives. This is accomplished through a re-sensitizing, a "tuning into" the spiritual dimension of our otherwise materialistic age in which technology has virtually replaced God.

Creating the conditions for this encounter has a specific name—*prayer*. Some have called this natural impulse of the human soul the very *breath* and *food* of the spirit. Unfortunately, this most important human experience is often reduced to a list of needs or to an eleventh hour appeal to powers that are otherwise considered irrelevant to our lives. True prayer is something else. The next chapter presents the experiences of men and women who discovered prayer as encounter with the sacred.

IV

Prayer as Encounter

THE ESSENCE OF PRAYER

The only true joy on earth is to escape from the prison of our own false self, and enter by love into union with the Life Who dwells and sings within the essence of every creature and in the core of our own souls.(1)

Thomas Merton was aware of the inward crisis of our time and of the great need for deep prayer. He understood that the moral evil in the world is due to our alienation from the spiritual life within us. Prayer, then, is ultimately a "consciousness of one's union with God."(2)

The problem for many seekers today is that they remain unaware of the "presence of the infinite source of being right in the midst of the world."(3) Prayer is meant to open our hearts to God by enabling us to surrender our inmost depths to the divine presence within us.

According to the great men and women of the inner life, prayer is a response to God's love for us. In the following pages, I will bring together central insights from some of the recognized masters in the field of spirituality and prayer.

They all point to the fact that prayer is ultimately a matter of experiencing the presence of the Transcendent.

The Quaker author Douglas Steere described prayer in

this way:

> The prayer of devotion is a response, a reply, the only appropriate reply that a man or a woman could make who had been aware of the love at the heart of things.(4)

For Steere, prayer is simply a form of waking up out of the dull sleep in which our life has been spent. He writes that in the most real prayer of all there occurs a refocusing of our life until it is brought to abide in Divine Love.

> At those moments a man comes to recognize the distinction between his praying and his being *prayed in.* Unless you are ready and willing to seek that kind of inner empathy and submit to that kind of inner renovation, it would be better not to play at praying.(5)

M. Basil Pennington, the popular author and monk, describes prayer as liberation. He agrees with Merton that there is danger that our prayers can get between us and God. "The great thing is not to pray, but to go directly to God."(6) The French monk Henry Le Saux, who became deeply involved with Hindu mysticism, believes that the aim of prayer is not to form concepts of God, however lofty they may be. "It is for God Himself, for God beyond any sign and any veil, that the soul, fed by the Gospel and the Spirit, is thirsty."(7) Echoing the perception of all the great mystics and saints, Le Saux affirms that the real place of the divine encounter is in the center of our being, the place of our origin, from which all that we are is continually welling up.

For the noted theologian Karl Barth, to be a Christian and to pray are the same thing. Barth reminds us that if we pray with the whole heart, we have the assurance that, however inadequate our words and our methods may be, God will hear and respond.(8)

The Jewish philosopher Abraham Heschel tells us that prayer is the means of transformation and transcendence of the self.

"All life must be a training to pray. We pray the way we live."(9)

In the *Philokalia*, we find practical guidance for the achieving of such a prayer life. The process begins with the benign energy of attention as a way of encountering the Divine. "Attention means cutting off thoughts, it is the abode of remembrance of God and the treasure-house of the power to endure all that may come. Therefore attention is the origin of faith, hope and love."(10)

These texts remind us that we must put before all else the universal commandment to remember God: "Thou shalt remember the Lord thy God" (Deuteronomy 7:18). Through the ancient tradition of the Prayer of the Heart, or the Jesus Prayer, one learns to combine attention centered in the moment with a state of ceaseless prayer. But the first condition of any further development is for the beginner to know himself and the complex labyrinth of his or her psychological make-up. This means becoming aware of our obstacles to communion with God.

This beginning point is common to all the great teachers of prayer. For the act of praying is not so much an effort on our part as it is a manifestation and flowering of God's grace in us. The purpose of human effort is to clear away the obstacles to this manifestation. We are then involved in the discovery of our true identity beneath the masks we wear and the defenses we have built up. In the process of dying to this artificial self, we can begin to live from a deeper center within, where the Eternal is encountered. This God-consciousness is the essence of experiencing religion as transformation. The Quaker author Thomas Kelly gives us a hint of what this new way of life implies:

What is here urged are internal practices and habits of the mind. What is here urged are secret habits of unceasing orientation of the deeps of our being about the Inward Light, ways of conducting our inward life so that we are perpetually bowed in worship while we are also busy in the world of daily affairs. This practice is the heart of religion.(11)

Kelly further emphasizes the fact that at some point along this journey to becoming, we discover that prayer is much more than techniques, concentration, and surrender:

For though we begin the practice of secret prayer with a strong sense that we are the initiators and that by our wills we are establishing our habits, maturing experience brings awareness of being met and tutored, purged and disciplined, simplified and made pliant in His holy will by a power waiting within us. For God Himself works in our souls, in their deepest depths, taking increasing control as we are progressively willing to be prepared for His wonder.(12)

Thomas Merton asserts that the life of prayer is founded on the prayer of petition (asking) no matter what it may develop into later on. He observes that as we become less aware of ourselves and more aware of God within us, petitionary prayer yields to other levels such as thanksgiving, praise and adoration. "In these latter types of prayer man is no longer concerned with himself but with God."(13) Evelyn Underhill points out the implications of intercessory prayer (prayers for the welfare of others):

It implies first our implicit realization of God, the infinitely loving, living and all-penetrating Spirit of Spirits, as an Ocean in which we all are bathed. And next, that somehow through this uniting and vivifying medium we too, being one with Him in love and will, can mutually penetrate, move and influence each other's souls in ways as yet unguessed.(14)

Underhill reminds us that it is partly through the prayerful actions of human beings that the spiritual work of this world is done. "When a man or a woman of prayer, through their devoted concentration, reaches a soul in temptation and rescues it, we must surely acknowledge that this is the action of God Himself, using that person as an instrument."(15) She adds that if we are to love people irrespective of merit or opinion or personal preference—which is essential to real intercession—we continually feed and maintain "the temper of adoration and trustful adherence,"(16) which is the heart of the life of prayer. In a letter to a friend, Thomas Merton reveals his way of experiencing such prayer:

Strictly speaking I have a very simple way of prayer. It is centered entirely on attention to the presence of God and to his will and to his love. That is to say that it is centered on faith by which alone we can know the presence of God. My prayer is then a kind of praise rising up out of the center of Nothingness and Silence. If I am still present *myself*, this I recognize as an obstacle. If he wills, he can then make the Nothingness into total clarity.(17)

THE PRACTICE OF PRAYER

Retreat leader and professor Grace Brame, in her work *Receptive Prayer*, offers a clear expression of the practice and purpose of prayer. The various definitions of prayer referred to above can essentially be grouped together under Ms. Brame's term "receptive prayer." She defines this receptive prayer as a means of becoming "in tune with the Infinite." She further defines this tuning and binding as coming through:

A relaxation of the body in God's presence,

A dedication of the will to God,

A focusing of the mind on God,

A receptivity to the Spirit of God, and

A sharing of the Gift of God.(18)

Appealing to our empirical and scientific view of reality, the author observes that our state of mind can and does stimulate the pituitary gland which, through the production of hormones, directs and affects the whole body. This process also causes the flow of endorphins and enkephalins which are protein substances manufactured in the body as natural pain killers. More importantly, the attitude created and reinforced by receptive prayer is one of being positive, hopeful, trusting, and expectant. Brame states that receptive prayer is a holistic way of praying whose results are far beyond superstitious or mechanical prayer. "The one who prays accepts the responsibility of being part of the answering process, of even finding the answer in the almost wholly undiscovered world within himself."(19) This sort of prayer is not a coaxing of the divine, but rather a receiving of what God already has in store for us. This receptivity allows us to be instructed and to accept the reality of grace and its transforming power.

After a relaxing of the body and a focusing of the mind, the next absolutely essential step is the Prayer of Commitment to God. It is a form of directed yielding to God's creative change. A period of "soaking in" follows when we are receptive to the love and peace or presence surrounding us. Then other gifts may be received: perhaps guidance for a problem posed or understanding of a person who is either loved or disliked. Here we intercede for others by sharing in spirit with them or by being taught to understand their needs . . . We have centered in order to expand outwards. Receptive Prayer is not selfish. In giving ourselves to God, we are more able to give ourselves to others.(20)

This way of praying is a pathway of revelation. Through this form of prayer we both receive and transmit information, energy, and emotion. We become a channel for God's grace, an expression of incarnate love. "It is God who does the work, but He is not just "out there somewhere," but in and through us and His creation."(21) The highest use of receptive prayer is to allow God to permeate our being.

This form of Christian meditation is different from secular or manipulative uses of meditation adapted for positive thinking, relaxation, and concentration. Receptive prayer has much in common with the meditation of other religions, particularly Buddhism, Hinduism, and Sufism. Their common goal is "an openness to God-centered commitment and contact, and a willingness to rest upon, release, and yield to God so that we can be more completely his, enabling his creation to continue in us and his creativity to flow through us."(22)

Receptive prayer is essentially one of inward silence in which the soul waits patiently to feel the Divine presence. When one enters such prayer, the attitude must be that of knowing that one is placing oneself in the presence of the Holy. From this consciousness comes a strength of attention and a capacity to yield and thus receive whatever is given. Our work is to endeavor to bring peace and silence into our mind and heart.

We are then to maintain a state of humble watchfulness. This effort is difficult at first because we have virtually no control over our power of attention. The saints tell us that our wandering imagination is permitted in order to exercise our patience, prove our faithfulness, and reveal how little we can do on our own. We then learn to depend on a greater Power.

We are told that if we faithfully persevere, every obstacle

will gradually be removed and inward silence will become easier. It is primarily because of the lack of this inward recollection that we are so rarely aware of the Divine Light. It should therefore become our daily practice because the more we practice silent prayer, the more we desire it.

STAGES OF PRAYER

Father Pennington suggests three rules that synthesize and simplify hundreds of years of wisdom on the practice of prayer.

Rule One: At the beginning of the prayer, take a minute or two to quiet down and then move in faith to God dwelling in your depths; and at the end of the prayer take several minutes to come out of our inner sanctuary.

Rule Two: After resting for a time in the center of your being, take up a single, simple word that expresses your response to this encounter and begin to let it repeat itself within.

Rule Three: Whenever in the course of the prayer you become aware of anything else, simply return to the prayer word.(23)

The nineteenth century French priest and author, Jean-Nicholas Grou, whose book *How to Pray* is a classic in the field, offers us a more specific set of principles:

1. We must be taught inwardly.
2. God alone teaches.

3. Prayer is a supernatural act beyond our strength.

4. Preparation consists in detachment and quietness of heart.

5. Begin with confession of insufficiency.

6. We must perform it in tranquility under the Spirit's guidance.

7. God listens to the voice of the heart.

8. Keep attention fixed on God's presence.

9. Pure adoration is simple attention of the mind.

10. Respect what cannot be understood.

11. God's action is to keep us in a state of holy calm in His presence.

12. The essential aim of all prayer is the glory of God.

13. To a soul that has made some progress, love is not a matter of feeling, but rather the determination of the will to do everything and to suffer everything for God.

14. God answers purity of intention and disposition of the heart.(24)

Thomas Kelly names the depths of prayer *inward listening.*

Prayer is a two-way process. It is not just human souls whispering to God. It passes over into communion, with God active in us, as well as we active toward God. A specific state of expectancy, of openness of soul is laid bare and receptive before the Eternal Goodness. In quietness we wait, inwardly, in unformulated expectation. (25)

Merton insists that we need not strain and strive after spiritual encounter through prayer. The Spirit is already with us. It is simply a matter of giving it a chance to make itself known to us. Spiritual directors of all ages have therefore offered these basic counsels to persons seeking God through prayer:

1. Do not wait until you feel like praying or you will stop praying when you need it most.
2. To desire to pray is already a result of prayer.
3. Know that God is waiting for you.
4. Never forget that the less you pray, the more you do it poorly.

THE HEART OF PRAYER

The heart of prayer is to forget ourselves and our interests so as to listen attentively. If we become uncentered, it is important to immediately turn again gently and peacefully inward. Prayer is not confined to our appointed times. Ancient texts tell us that it is especially important to seek nothing from our Creator, but to simply desire to please God and do God's will.

> Go, then, to prayer not that ye may enjoy spiritual delights, but that ye may be full or empty, just as it pleaseth God. This will preserve you in an evenness of spirit, either in desertion or in consolation, and will prevent your being surprised at dryness, or the

apparent repulses of Him who is altogether love.(26)

Constant prayer, unceasing prayer, requires that we keep our heart always right toward God. True religion is an emanation of truth and goodness within the soul of a human being, where we eventually partake in the Divine nature. Douglas Steere tells of the last words of a much-loved professor of philosophy in Germany to his students who asked him to give them a parting message. This is what he sent them from his deathbed:

> The magic key is not reflection, as you might expect from a philosopher, but it is prayer. Prayer as the most complete act of devotion makes us quiet, makes us objective. A man grows in true humanity in prayer. Prayer is the final humility of the spirit. The greatest things in existence will only be given to those who pray. In suffering one learns to pray best of all.(27)

Bernard of Clairvaux, the celebrated monk of the twelfth century, shares in this way his profound devotional experience, expressing that particularly Christian dimension of humility:

> Although He has frequently entered my soul, I have never at any time been sensible of the precise moment of His coming. I have felt that He was present; I remember that He has been with me; I have sometimes been able even to have a presentiment that He would come; but never to feel His coming or His departure. For whence He came to enter my soul, or whither He went on quitting it, by what means He has made entrance or departure, I confess that I know not, even

to this day.(28)

Douglas Steere speaks of the loss of oneself which suddenly leads one into a deeper and vaster encounter with Reality:

> How good to remember how in prayer one day my stiff, tight, detailed petitions were all blown aside as though they were dandelion fluff, how I stopped praying and began to be prayed in, of how I died and was literally melted down by the love of a Power that coursed through my heart sweeping away the hard claimful core, and poured through me a torrent of infinite tenderness and caring!(29)

Ignatius of Loyola insists at the end of his classic manual that all exercises are nothing but preparation for the prayer of affection (silent love) and should drop away if and when it comes, as a lamp is turned off when the sun comes up. At its deepest levels, prayer becomes a simple, loving response to the creative love of God. Will, intellect, emotion are no longer involved, but the very ground of our being, the root of existence enters into spiritual communion with God. Meister Eckhart left us with these words:

> One should learn to work with this contemplation in him, with him, and emerging from him, so that one allows his inner life to break into his activity and his activity into his inner life so that one becomes accustomed to working collectedly. If they can both happen in him, that is best of all, for then he becomes a fellow workman with God.(30)

There are certain basic elements that must be present in the preparation of turning to God. We will need quiet and solitude for the practice of prayer. This is not to say that a quiet mind cannot be found in the midst of a crowd, but such a capacity to *seal oneself* from the distractions of the senses is a gift and a discipline that are rarely achieved. We must begin with God, not with ourselves when we pray. Brother Lawrence speaks to us of "practicing the presence of God." This simply means to live intentionally in God's presence, and to be conscious of living in this presence. He took seriously the words of Jesus: "I am with you always" (Matthew 28:20). Love is the key to practicing or experiencing the presence of God. Our relationship with God is one of love, and because we love God we are eager to be in our Creator's presence. Thus the love of God becomes the purpose and goal of all our actions. When we know that God is with us all the time, we live for God alone. We place ourselves entirely in God's hands that God may do with us and through us what God wills. Thomas Kelly learned the practice of the presence of God in this way:

> The first days and weeks and months are awkward and painful, but enormously rewarding. Awkward because it takes constant vigilance and effort and reassertions of the will, at the first level. Painful because our lapses are so frequent, the intervals when we forget Him so long. Rewarding, because we have begun to live. But these weeks and months and perhaps even years must be passed through before He gives us greater and easier stayedness upon Himself.(31)

This practice is certainly not easy and requires every ounce of will power, effort, and self-sacrifice of which we are capable. Yet we cannot tell anyone how to live in the presence of God. We can only point out that we begin by becoming receptive to spiritual presence and accepting the movements of grace. Our work is never to give up and always to begin again. This translates into dying to oneself and offering our soul to God. Our work includes inner efforts that ancient Christian tradition called *mortification*. This term has been terribly misunderstood and has led to pathological distortions. Through a synthesizing of some of the great writers on prayer, Evelyn Underhill makes the following observations concerning mortification:

1. Quietly to suffer all crosses, difficulties, and contradictions to self-will, whether internal or external, including temptations and dryness (lack of emotional longing for God).

2. Never to do or omit things on account of one's likes or dislikes, but to refer everything to God's will.

3. Those mortifications are right for us which increase humility and power of prayer and are performed with cheerful resolution. They are wrong if deliberately undertaken instead of the obvious difficulties of life and if they produce depression and strain.

4. Habitual quietness of mind is essential to true mortification. All impetuosity and unquietness has in it some self-love, but the Holy Spirit is stillness, serenity, and peace.

5. In general, the mortifications sent by God and the

ordinary friction of existence are enough to discipline our souls. Voluntary mortifications are never to be assumed until the necessary difficulties and contradictions of life are cheerfully and fully accepted.(32)

THE EXAMINATION OF CONSCIENCE

The men and women of former centuries who dedicated their lives to communion with God found that they could not hope to participate in such an accomplishment without great effort. The maxim which states that nothing important is free applies especially to the spiritual life.

Various religious traditions suggest that we begin with writing down our daily schedules. It might include devotional readings, prayer, and service. Some moments are spent in quiet contemplation, thanksgiving, and offering our day to God. If we can find a few minutes during the day, prayers of intercession for specific persons may be offered up. Evenings are important for prayer, if they occur before we are too tired. This time of prayer can be the longest of the day and include the examination of conscience. This is an ancient practice counseled by centuries of spiritual directors. In his luminous work, *Where Silence Dwells*, Alphonse Goettmann shares the steps of this ancient practice:

1) Give thanks for the blessings received during the day. The importance of this fundamental attitude cannot be overly stressed as it is the beginning of all true discernment. We have received the Spirit and its gifts and it is the spirit of joy which is suffocated if we

are always displeased with ourselves, with others and with our life. Joy and gratitude should be the general atmosphere of the soul and must always be renewed, awakened, and deepened. But later we must give thanks for concrete and personal gifts that have come during the day. Nothing is to be taken for granted and nothing is owed us: light, health, the air that we breathe, a child's laughter, a loved one's joy, a colleague's handshake, our work, our home.

2) Ask God for the light to know the movements that have led you. In prayer, we must try to read past our feelings, desires, repulsions, impulses, or blockages to what the signs are that the Spirit is making to us, how it leads us, toward what it constantly attracts us. This is a thread which goes through all our activities and is found beneath our psychic life and the movements of the soul. This is a discernment which needs to be continually refined.

3) Look at your thoughts, words, and needs, not as a detailed review, but for the sake of becoming conscious of what has occurred to you and in you during the day. The essential question is: how did the Creator engender me today (Psalm 2:7) from thought to thought, action to action? What work did God accomplish in me? At the very heart of our spontaneous feelings, God leads us and deals with us in the most intimate way. These movements are studied in order to discern from what spirit they come. Little by little, we learn to listen and to feel in every moment how God knocks at our door:

love is played out minute by minute in very precise acts.

4) Ask forgiveness of God. The aim here is to learn that we are forgiven sinners. Nothing builds up praise more than this knowledge. Ask God to forgive us our many betrayals of love. Forgive others, love them as they are. Forgive events that are contrary to you, accept them, even when unacceptable; love (that is, *bless*) your enemies under whatever form they appear. Recurring forgiveness increasingly leads to a state of forgiveness, and the ego slowly disappears along with the tyranny of emotions. This leads to a stability in the soul that gives birth one day to serenity, the sign of supreme freedom and of a joy that does not depend on external events.

5) In the light of the discernment that you have just done, how do you now see the future? Let the attitude live in you that you would like to have tomorrow, at work, under a certain circumstance or encounter. Then entrust yourself to God and surrender yourself to Him. It is He who will live through you.(33)

THE ASCENT OF THE SOUL

Classical devotion theology has told us that the ascent of the soul occurs through the threefold ladder of *purgation, illumination,* and *union.* This book cannot enter into a study of such voluminous material, but it will address one aspect of human experience that runs through the entire "ascent," namely spiritual dryness, also known as *the dark night of the soul.* These are times when there seems to be no response from God and no renewal of courage or inspiration or sense of God's presence. The causes are many—physical fatigue, imbalances in our glandular activity, and moods that we have long indulged in such as self-pity, melancholia, general irritation. These empty, dry times also remind us of the fact that we are not capable of dwelling permanently in higher altitudes where the presence of the sacred is known. We are finite beings and will not know the Divine face to face until the flesh has been left behind. Yet we must remember that prayer is not simply our own activity but involves a living relationship between the infinite transcendent and the finite transient. Times of dryness are means by which God continues the work of dissolving our self-centeredness. This is a purification of the self, wherein the center of focus in our lives shifts from self to God. This is a time when true self-surrender is called for, when our reliance on God's guidance and goodness comes from an intuition that is supported only by the most subtle of feelings. Thus we grow as we give way to God and offer to our Maker all that we are and have and do. Father Jean-Pierre De Caussade, the seventeenth century spiritual director and author of a little masterpiece called *The Sacrament of the Present Moment*, left us with this wisdom:

> Since we know that divine action understands, directs and creates everything apart from sin, we must love and worship all it does, welcoming it with open arms. In joy and confidence we must override everything in order to bring about the triumph of faith . . . To live by faith, then, is to live in joy, confidence, certainty and trust in

all there is to do and suffer each moment as ordained by God. However mysterious it may seem, it is in order to awaken and maintain this living faith that God drags the soul through tumultuous floods of so much suffering, trouble, perplexity, weariness, and ruin. For faith is needed to discover in all this God and that divine life which can neither be seen nor felt but, nevertheless, in some mysterious way, unmistakably reveals itself.(34)

De Caussade tells us further that the love of God and submission to the divine will is all that is required. Here are timeless words born out of the discovery of inner treasures:

You will never know either from whence you come or where you are going, from what purpose of God divine wisdom has taken you and to where it is leading you. All that remains for you to do is passively to surrender yourselves . . . acting when it is the moment to act, ceasing when it is the moment to cease, losing when it is the moment to lose . . . And, after many transformations, perfected, your souls will receive wings to fly up to heaven, having sown on earth the fertile seed of their state of self-surrender to live in others forever.(35)

This process of transformation is the goal of the religious life. The aim of all the methods of prayer is to make possible the emergence of divine light shining clearly and without interruption. The soul is then led into a clear vision of God. The path to the depths of prayer involves both self-discovery and self-surrender. The devotional lives of the men and women quoted here reveal to us the most direct way to an attainment of the consciousness of our spiritual environment which the mystics call the *Presence of God*. It is our birthright to achieve a simple kind of contemplation that opens onto such life-giving awareness. But after all the wisdom has been learned and the techniques tested, we must remember the conclusion of a mystic of the seventeenth century: "The greatest method in prayer is to have none." This paradox is resolved by the profound observation of Augustine, one of the greatest teachers of the western Church: "We come to God by love and not by navigation."

PART TWO

Open the door and let yourself be found.
That is the whole thing.

—Karlfried Graf Dürckheim

V

The Depths of Sacred Text

The early Christians were clear that any real understanding of the Scriptures began with the state of the reader—the reading itself is a spiritual event. Depending on one's receptivity, sensitivity to intuitive guidance, alertness, and detachment from distractions, religious texts can become a source of stunning insight. Their power does not come from reading done with the intellect alone, but from the presence of the whole person focused on the message of the text.

I have experienced powerful moments through the encounter with a few words or a sentence of scripture. These readings have often come at a critical moment and seem to be *accidental* in that I had not intended to read them at the time. But they were immediately applicable to the situation at hand and directly affected its outcome. Clearly, the emotional, mental and spiritual state in which one finds oneself in the moment of reading makes all the difference. The words themselves are merely the tip of the iceberg. The encounter with the Spirit at the juncture of text and reader is the reason why such material is called sacred.

There are, nevertheless, certain issues important to studying the record of these teachings. In the long run, the following "historical-critical" knowledge does not have the power to interfere with a reader's search for the divine. But as we so often approach things through the intellect, it is helpful to keep the following elements in mind.

DATE AND PLACE OF COMPOSITION

Many sacred writings, and the Bible in particular, came down to us originally by oral transmission and then through centuries of copying, re-copying, and translations of these copies. We are far from the original words uttered by Christ. In fact, nothing was put to paper until some forty years after the events described in the New Testament had taken place.

Let us take the case of the Gospel of John, called by many the "spiritual gospel." The earliest papyri in existence, the Ryland Papyrus P52 found in Egypt, is placed at the beginning of the second century. As it is generally supposed that the author of the gospel knew the writer of the gospel of Luke, the date of composition of the fourth gospel is thought to be as early as 80 A.D. Other scholars believe that it predates the other gospels and may have been written as early as 44 A.D.

Syria is a probable location for the writing because of the Semitic character of the Greek sentence structures in the gospel. Egypt is also considered a possible place of composition, particularly because of the parallels between the ideas of the philosopher Philo and the prologue of the gospel.

PURPOSE AND STYLE

The purpose of the author of the Gospel of John is connected to the community of which he was a part. He was concerned with legitimizing the particular form of Christianity that distinguished his group. Some scholars believe that the fourth gospel reflects the final stages of the new religion's separation from its Jewish roots, and the expulsion of Christians from the synagogues may have served as motivation for writing the text. Other scholars suggest that the literary unity of the gospel implies the existence of a *school*, possibly in the tradition of the Pythagorean School or the Essene communities. Again, they point to the separation between Christians who remained adherents of official Judaism and those who were inspired by the rich thought of Greek philosophy.

The environment out of which the so-called Johannine community appeared was that of the esoteric circles of Palestinian Judaism. Parallels have been drawn between the Gospel of John and gnosticism. The little known Samaritan religion also fed into this syncretism which is one of the sources of early Christianity.

In his work *The Birth of Christianity*, Maurice Goguel tells us that the gospel passed through several stages before reaching the form in which we know it. He concludes that it consequently lost "some of its freshness" and was gradually adapted to the general mind and needs of the Church.(1) Goguel finds that the author's thoughts are not so much elements of a system as the record of experiences, the expression of mystic intuitions.

The noted scholar Johannes Weiss writes that the greatness of the author's style is that he understands how to suggest the inexpressible, how to set the mind of his readers to "vibrating in unison with the tones which he sounds, and to expand their inner consciousness with the mystery of their religion."(2) It is generally agreed in academic circles that the gospel as a whole is the result of a complex process spread over a period of many years.

TRANSLATIONS

For our purposes here, I will briefly compare translations of the gospel taken from the *Revised Standard Version* Bible and the *French Jerusalem* Bible. The RSV translates the well-known verse nine of the first chapter of John as follows: "The true light that enlightens every man was coming into the world." The Jerusalem Bible reads: "Le Verbe était la lumière véritable, qui éclaire tout homme." (The Verb was the true light that enlightens every man). The latter translation has the predicate stating that the "Verb" (or "Word" in the English version, which in itself is an interesting difference in meaning) was the true light, whereas the RSV makes "light" the subject with "true" as adjective rather than direct object. A literal translation of the Greek New Testament reads: "The light the true one was, which enlightens every man coming into the world." Here are the three versions back to back:

The true light that enlightens every man was coming into the world.   —*Revised Standard Version*

The Verb was the true light that enlightens every man
    —*Jerusalem Bible*

The light the true one was, which enlightens every man
coming into the world. —*Greek New Testament*

The above are subtle differences and presented here only as
an example that can be multiplied countless times through
the Old and New Testaments. Emphasis, tone, use of
synonyms and grammatical structure all have an impact on
the meaning of the text. Interpretation then becomes very
subjective and relative, which accounts in part for the
shattering of Christendom into thousands of sects and
denominations. Another example of this problem is found in
verse 14:2: "In my Father's house are many rooms; if it were
not so, would I have told you that I go to prepare a place for
you?"

Most translators believe that these heavenly dwellings
are of the kind mentioned in Jewish and gnostic texts. But
the early Fathers saw them as degrees of heavenly perfection
while others understood the "many dwellings" as
"indwelling" and therefore as spiritual union without
reference to heaven or the afterlife whatsoever. These
dwellings may be located in the believers themselves who live
in the world. Some scholars find this idea confirmed in the
Gospel of Thomas, whose sayings are as old as any of those
recorded in the New Testament. "He said to them: you too
seek for yourselves a place within for rest" (saying 60).

For people who turn to scripture in search of life-giving
and transforming insight, this situation is sometimes
discouraging. It then becomes necessary to seek out the inner

meaning of these writings, based on one's own inspiration of the moment and on an intuitive understanding of their spiritual symbolism.

DECODING SYMBOLS AND PARABLES

One of the finest interpreters of the inner, psychological meaning of religious teachings is Maurice Nicoll. He was a brilliant English psychologist, an associate of C.G. Jung, and later became an acclaimed teacher of the Gurdjieff system of inner work that is described in chapter seven. Nicoll wrote two books on this crucial subject, *The New Man* and *The Mark*, that are, unfortunately, as little known as the man himself. Yet they are striking in their uncovering of practical, empowering material at the heart of the teachings. His approach, which is close to the ancient allegorical method of the early Fathers and mystics, solves the dilemma caused by the issues mentioned above. Rather than quibbling over possible definitions of words that are themselves questionable in relation to the original source, Nicoll takes us directly to the heart of the matter. His interpretations are grounded in universal spiritual symbolism that are applicable to all the great religious texts and deal with genuine human transformation.

Nicoll tells us that a parable is a medium of connection between a lower and a higher meaning. He suggests that, in the language of parables, everything on earth represents something belonging to our understanding. In other words, objects become ideas or psychological meanings. It is not the visual imagery or the words in the parable that are important, for they are only conductors of meaning. This is why any literal interpretation is wrong or at least limiting from the very outset.

Most of us can never hope to fully plumb the depths of scripture. The issue of the symbolism of numbers alone is a lifetime study. For example, the recurring numbers 3, 12, and 40 all come from highly sophisticated Jewish mysticism and encompass vast meaning. Nicoll tells us that the destruction of higher (inner and psychological) truth by literal truth is the continual drama of human life. If we can tune into the spirit of the text by preparing ourselves to be inspired by the same Spirit that inspired the writers and the events described, then perhaps scripture will not only come alive, but make us come alive as well.

Nicoll offers us a dynamic approach and time honored encounter with scripture. He eradicates most of the obstacles that stand in the way of making the Bible meaningful for modern people. He presents us with a radical insight into the word *metanoia* which he translates as "metamorphosis of the mind" rather than "repentance." He tells us that "everything appears suddenly in a new light, something makes one understand that all that is happening in life is not the important thing, but what is important is one's attitude." (3)

Nicoll understands the idea of "the Kingdom of Heaven," for instance, as a higher possibility within ourselves. Only the individual can take the first step on the journey of development that leads to the state of "rebirth." Along with the early teachers of "the Way" (the original name of Christianity), Nicoll reminds us that we live both in and outside of time. If nothing is transformed beyond the sensory level, we live primarily in time. How much of us is outside time and space depends on how much we can organize inner space through positive states of consciousness and keep this place separate from the jarring of everyday events. This is the "room" in which we are told to go and pray.

Nicoll offers us a brilliant analogy that sheds new light on an old story: an Ark must be built to survive the flood pouring in from the outer senses. Our Arks must be seaworthy as it takes a long time (forty days and forty nights) before the evidence of things not seen is stronger than the evidence of things seen. God's existence is known and experienced through the development of these states of awareness.

Another such interpreter of the scriptures is Father Alphonse Goettmann, a priest in the Orthodox Church of France. His approach is entirely rooted in the deep spirituality of early Christianity as taught by the Fathers. He asserts that we are in the world to become transformed. This is a mutation of being, not a simple moral improvement. It requires a death to one reality in order to be reborn into another. Father Goettmann offers us the following parable of the grain as a contemporary expression of the depth of teaching within the biblical stories.

A CONTEMPORARY PARABLE

The grain of wheat is happy in its barn. It's not too cold, not too hot. What more could we want besides the joy of health, achievement, and comfort? All is well. But these are tiny pleasures and if we remain with them, we will miss the meaning of life. God did not create us for that alone.

One day, the grain is tossed with many others onto a wagon, in search of more pleasures. This is a whole new life: a resplendent sun, a blue sky, birds and trees. Life is beautiful, God is good. But the grain remains an untransformed grain. In the midst of pleasure, its life is a failure. The wagon finally comes to freshly plowed earth. The sower places the grain deep in the soil. This is an unexpected trial: humidity enters into its core and it freezes in the darkness. Depression and illness come along. It decomposes and is going to die. Even its faith in God tumbles into dust, for the grain says to itself, "If God existed, this would not be happening to me."

Winter passes, as do all winters, and the grain finally accepts this incomprehensible hardship, surrendering itself entirely to the fertile soil. In the very depths of its tomb, it suddenly feels a strange surge. An entirely different Life begins to grow at the heart of its acceptance. In discovering that Someone is at work behind all this, the grain of wheat even manages to say "yes" to all that happens to it, becoming one with the earth and the trial that is imposed on it. Every time the grain does this, it dies a little more to itself and to all its prejudices concerning happiness. Then it notices a fullness rising within. One spring day, while its whole being gives thanks in this night within the earth, a surprising fullness breaks through. It rises above the earth, overcoming all obstacles. The grain is transformed into an ear of corn.

Once again, it joins its song with the sun, the sky, the birds and trees, but it is no longer for the same reasons. It has now understood why it exists and where the joy is found that no one can take away.(4)

* * *

This modern parable clearly expresses the fact that it is a metaphor for a spiritual process. Understanding parables in this way uncovers enormous new material in the scriptures. Consider Nicoll's interpretation of Christ's parable of the sower:

"A sower went out to sow. And as he sowed, some seeds fell along the path, and the birds came and devoured them. Other seeds fell on rocky ground, where they had not much soil, and immediately they sprang up, since they had no depth of soil, but when the sun rose they were scorched; and since they had no root they withered away. Other seeds fell upon thorns, and the thorns grew up and choked them. Other seeds fell on good soil and brought forth grain, some a hundredfold, some sixty, some thirty. He who has ears, let him hear." (Matthew 13:3)

The seed that is sown into the earth is both the human being and the teaching of the possible inner evolution to a higher level called *Heaven*. When the teachings are not understood, the birds come an devour them. These birds represent our thoughts (Nicoll observes that Plato called the human mind a bird cage). When the seed is "trodden underfoot" it means that the ideas are taken literally, with the natural mind. The four kinds of ground—way side, rocky, chocked by thorns, good ground—describe four ways of receiving and understanding the teaching on inner evolution. They represent states of consciousness. The first category, way side, represents those who cannot overcome the merely literal, sense-based understanding of the teaching; rocky ground represents those who take in the teaching superficially, merely as knowledge. Nicoll points out that, in the symbolic language of parable, "rock" represents a primitive level of Truth that cannot quench one's thirst. Thorns represent those who are choked by self-interest and whose will cannot make room for the teaching. They cannot live by the revealed Truth because of other interests. Good ground represents those who see the value of the teaching, apply it to themselves, and bring it to fruition. They become this fruition through their own inner evolution. As with all spiritual imagery, there are multiple dimensions of insight to be uncovered. For these categories do not only represent different kinds of persons or different ways of receiving Truth, but also different levels of development in the same person. If we go back and read the parable with these ideas in mind, we will find new meaning in every sentence that is immediately applicable to our lives.

One final example of the symbolic expression of religious teaching: the image of the master washing the disciples' feet. We can certainly appreciate it for its expression of humble service to humanity. But Nicoll reveals a much deeper insight when he tells us that the ritual of washing feet refers to the cleansing of the natural mind (associated with feet, earth, literal understanding) from the illusions of appearances. We find a much more profound meaning in this interpretation that opens new vistas in the entire teaching of Jesus.

APPROACHING SACRED TEXT

I have found one of the finest teachings on reading scriptures in the book *Where Silence Dwells: Christian Wisdom and Practice* by Alphonse and Rachel Goettmann. They bring together the wisdom of the early Christian tradition and focus entirely on the ultimate purpose of the writings—the reader's transformation. The following guidelines and insights are translated here from this book for the first time. I believe they offer a holistic understanding for applying this method of spiritual encounter that has been part of the human experience for centuries. This is an approach based on ancient traditions for those who seek to read the Bible but lack a method to receive its spiritual contents. The Goettmanns begin their approach with a question and an observation that may resonate with many modern readers:

How many persons have aspired to read the Bible only to find the task impossible and put it aside in disappointment? Whatever hope they may have had to discover a mysterious and unknown land has encountered only indifference and emptiness, along with an incapacity to move any further into the reading. Where does this strange resistance come from? We do not enter into the Bible as we might with any other book.

THE BIBLE AS REAL PRESENCE

The Bible is where we find our Source. It is not a book or a document, but a *Revelation*: that of the Word that creates us in this moment, that maintains us in existence at each instant and shapes us toward the future. But there is infinitely more: as we listen, as our whole being becomes a receptive cup, this Word is made living and reveals itself as an always present Companion. It is Someone. The relationship which is established with the Bible is not at all that of subject and object, of the reader and the book, but a relation of love, of an *I* and a *You*, whose communion will someday bring forth a union. That is the meaning of the *Covenant*, which is the true name of the Bible. From then on, each "reading" of the Bible is in fact an invitation to an experience. The Gospel of John tells us: "Come and see" (John 1:39).

THE BOOK OF OUR TRANSFORMATION

The Word of God is alive because it is the living Christ. But as a word, it has the virtue of being able to penetrate us as a seed penetrates the earth, and there it germinates and develops in our depths as new life that will illuminate our whole being from within and conform us to Christ himself: "You have been born anew, not from perishable seed but of imperishable, through the living and abiding word of God" (1 Peter 1:23). The etymological meaning of "word" (*dabar* in Hebrew) is the depth of things, that which is hidden and which the word will reveal. It therefore awakens us to our identity and our true vocation, just as it carries all things in the universe to their ultimate fulfillment. This is the Jewish vision of the word, an acting and efficient power, a voice that manifests a presence, a desire for communion. Our intellectual approach to the Word, according to the Greek concept that seeks knowledge about God, is an attitude that objectifies and keeps things at a distance. We can be a fount of science concerning it, and yet have never encountered it.

Nevertheless, the reader can find himself or herself on the same wavelength as the texts themselves. We are given the prophetic grace of a radically new understanding of history, taken beyond a simple narrative or literal reading and placed there where things originate. Through inspiration, we can receive from the text a message that is not in the text and that will remain inexhaustible.

CONDITIONS OF A FRUITFUL READING

1. THE INVOCATION OF THE HOLY SPIRIT

Prayer is the preamble to the process. The whole Tradition teaches that as soon as we receive the Word in prayer, the Spirit communicates its experience to us. The Word becomes organic knowledge within us. But without the presence of the Spirit, nothing will take place; the text will be only a relic from a concluded past, with no more interest than the writings of ancient philosophers.

2. A SET RENDEZ-VOUS

After prayer comes the time of the reading itself. Guillaume de Saint-Thierry tells us in his *Golden Letter* (thirteenth century): "At set hours, we must give ourselves to a specific reading. Far from edifying the soul, a reading with no direction throws it into inconstancy." It is important to set both the time of our reading and its length. This discipline already opens the heart to the gift of self. If the Bible is truly a Presence for us, then this time will be an encounter.

3. *A CHOSEN TEXT*

It is unthinkable to open the Bible half-heartedly or flip through it according to our whims. Such a reading is not likely to bear fruit. It is true that in times of great decisions, when what is at stake is the crossing over to a new stage of life or a great turning point, we can, after long prayer, open the Bible and put our finger on the text that will truly be a help from heaven. Many saints have done this, but it remains the exception. There must be a method to the daily study of Scripture. Following a liturgical calendar is an excellent one: it allows us to be in communion with the great mysteries that are unfolding during the year.

Another way consists of simply reading the New Testament from beginning to end, a little every day, and starting over indefinitely. From the Old Testament, the Psalms should be our daily bread because this is praying with the very words of the Holy Spirit. For the rest, it will probably be easier to begin with the prophets, then Isaiah to Malachi, then the books for edification such as Toby, Job, the Song of Songs, and only then the historical books. Whoever says they do not have time could take only one verse per day and carry it with him, pondering it all day long. Saint Thérèse of Lisieux used to say: "I take a verse of

Scripture as a chicken takes a drop of water: she raises her beek and lets it descend slowly."

We will also come across obscure passages that we will not understand or that will leave us indifferent, but this is of no importance. We receive the text as it comes, for itself, without seeking anything for ourselves through emotional satisfaction. Heidegger stated: "Rather than to understand, we must let ourselves be taken." The Word takes root within us, creates a path and, transforming us from within, gives us an understanding that is not merely mental and that will progressively illuminate the texts with the very light of God.

4. TAKING THE TIME TO SAVOR A TEXT

The preceding steps lead us to the quality of the reading. We must know how to stop, then read and reread the text over and over again for a long time in order to savor it. Saint Gregory the Great (sixth century) speaks of the "rumination" of the Word until "our stomach contains the book and our entrails are full of it." This idea is also found in Ezekiel 10:1-11 and throughout the Jewish Tradition (see Psalm 118). This was the practice of all the early Fathers: the Word must penetrate the spirit, the soul and the body; this impregnation gave birth in them to an incessant meditation. They assimilated the Scriptures and the Scriptures assimilated them. This suggests a great perseverance in reading. Such an effort is truly the sign and the measure of our spiritual progress, for it expresses our hunger and thirst for the Word. Saint Jerome wrote that "perseverance engenders familiarity." Without regularity, nothing can take place in any area of endeavor: "In perseverance will you find your crowning" (Revelation 2:10). Long and frequent study of the Bible opens us to its spirit, its language, its forms of expressions, the fundamental attitudes that it suggests, and will end by penetrating right into our reflexes, even the unconscious ones, unveiling secret and hidden things to us. This is an immersion in the Word where we become one with it. The experience is indescribable as are all intimate encounters, but these manifestations always result in "peace, joy and love," the fruits of the spirit, the signs that we have descended into the heart, there where the immediate contact with God takes place and where we hear the voice of the Beloved. Then we come into silence, into a contemplative state. Every word of the Bible rises out of the abyss of Silence and returns toward an abyss of Silence, coming to us through the power of the Spirit. (15)

With this approach to religious texts, we come upon a language of transformation. We have left behind the world of blind faith, superstition, or inherited worldviews. We now enter into the realm of personal change. This is not a matter of morality or appropriate behavior but rather the breakthrough of a new understanding of ourselves that generates radically new priorities. We enter upon a new way of life without necessarily changing anything in our outer circumstances. This way is written in our hearts and has been with us from the beginning.

The next section presents practical information on the continual process of transformation that is the purpose of religion and of life.

VI

Transformation Through Self-Awareness

You and I are not simply men and women who pay our bills, bring up a family, experience joys and sorrows and finally pass away like a dream that suddenly ends. We are much more than this. In our bodies that grow old, our spirits are made in the image of the Creator. We are not simply our picture on our driver's license or our social security number. We are the spiritual children of the eternal Creator.

But we limit ourselves to our nationality, our gender, our age. Nationality, for instance, can be a very narrow and dangerous thing. The French national anthem has a verse in its chorus that says: "May an impure blood soak into our fields." And of course this impure blood is anyone who is not French. This is not the mindset of a child of God. Evelyn Underhill stated: "For practical purposes, we have agreed that sanity consists in sharing the hallucinations of our neighbors."

When we are quiet and alone, without distractions, we can taste another quality of life. We can discover a vision of spiritual reality. The poet William Blake put it this way: "To see a world in a grain of sand, heaven in a wild flower, hold infinity in the palm of your hand, and eternity in an hour." We have all known such brief moments, but usually we limit our awareness to the physical reality we see around us. We find in the Christian tradition a very strange saying: "Let the dead bury the dead." Surely these words do not refer to the dead in body, for a dead body cannot bury another one. Christ was speaking of the dead in soul. A perfectly healthy body can have a dead soul within it. And what is a dead soul? One that has closed itself off to the source of its being, with no spiritual sensitivity or understanding. How does this happen to us?

First, we take ourselves entirely for granted. Consider our emotions. When we feel depressed or angry, we simply believe that to be who we are. And yet we all have this recurring wheel of emotions that varies from the greatest excitement to the most morbid depression. According to whatever stimulus comes before us, to whatever happens in our outer life, the wheel turns and we have no choice but to manifest that emotion, however destructive and unpleasant it may be. It happens so quickly that we seem to have no option other than to turn into that emotion. And yet, we do have a choice. It is possible to separate ourselves from negative experiences and not to be tyrannized by them. For if we take these emotions for granted, we come under their rule. We then live in a petty world of reactions, founded on a consciousness focused only on ourselves.

One of the key insights in spiritual awakening is that it is we who attract our lives and bring so much misery upon ourselves. While it is true that we have no choice but to be subject to such emotions, we do have a choice as to how we respond to them. We can release them through violence and ugliness, or channel that energy into something positive and not let them have their way with us. The poet e. e. cummings put it this way: "To be nobody but yourself in a world that is doing its best night and day to make you everybody else means to fight the hardest battle which any human being can fight and never stop fighting." This struggle begins with our own uncontrolled reactions. For when someone speaks or behaves in a way that we resent, we usually respond with great bitterness and carry terrible memories of the person. But there is another way: we can notice that we are violent or bitter and that is different.

The observation of our state lets in light, a consciousness of what is inside of us so that we do not simply behave unconsciously and automatically. We can then recognize that no matter who is to blame for the circumstances, we are to blame for being negative. The cause is in ourselves and not in the other person, because we have a choice and a responsibility to the universe not to release the poisonous energies of negativity. We also need to realize that self-love blocks out the more unpleasant part of ourselves from our consciousness. Worse still, we project this dark side upon others. The faults that we dislike in others are most often found in ourselves as well.

Cleansing, then, requires that we honestly confront what we are like. Such observation does not place value judgments on what it witnesses. Otherwise we run the danger of falling into repression rather than discipline. Repression is ashamed of reality while discipline confronts and masters it. Repression says of such things as hate, anger and envy: "I could never have such feelings." Discipline says: "Yes, I do have those feelings at times, but I'm not going to let them run and ruin my life." The repressed person never accepts himself as he is but is always trying to hide everything that does not agree with the false image he has built up, and which he so desperately defends and cherishes. The disciplined person has accepted himself, because he knows that he is accepted by virtue of being alive.

INNER AWARENESS

Just as we must be aware of the great outer world, so must we develop an awareness of our inner world. There is a vast psychological country within us, with many dangerous neighborhoods as well as entryways into regenerating peace. We have travelled through them all. Each of us has been mean and hateful, which are dark places in our being. If we pay attention to where we are in ourselves, perhaps we won't fall so easily into those quicksands within us.

Why is it that we cannot seem to control our states? The philosophical and religious traditions have a name for these states and this name describes the reason why we have no control: they call it *sleep*. In the New Testament alone, we read: "Awake, O Sleeper, and arise from the dead and Christ shall give you light." In the letter to the Thessalonians, we find these words: "So then let us not sleep as others do, but let us keep awake." The apostle Paul says: "It is high time for you to wake out of sleep." And Christ is recorded as saying:

"Watch! Do not sleep."

Certainly what is meant here is not literal sleep, but the self-centered consciousness that keeps us from experiencing that liberation called by so many names: "the Kingdom of Heaven," *Satori*, "cosmic consciousness," or even "peak experiences." As different as we are now from when we were sleeping in our beds, so is that state of self-centeredness different from the possible state that we can all attain.

AWAKENING

Consider this description of a state of sleep: you wake up one morning from an unpleasant dream, getting out on the wrong side of bed as they say, so you are rather grumpy. You go outside and find that the paper boy has thrown the paper into a mud puddle. A bad mood sets in. Your spouse rises late and you resent him or her because they suddenly seem to you like a lazy bum.

You decide to go out for a walk. The sun makes you feel better, you relax. You notice an accident down the road. It reminds you of an accident you were involved in last year coming home from a birthday party. Boy, that was a wonderful cake. Say, there's a cake back home that you suddenly feel like eating. You go home and have your coffee cake, and life is beautiful. You then remember a call you have to make. You dial the wrong number and some angry person tells you that you're a fool. Anger sets in and you should hear the way you speak to your children when they ask you if they can go play outside.

This takes place all day long. We associate from one

thing to another, bouncing off the stimulus that we encounter in every moment. Where is the freedom in such a person so overwhelmed by people and events and subject to such variations of temperament? This is the state of sleep.

We believe that we can change our lives through changing our outer circumstances. But as long as we remain as we are, we will attract the same problems and the same difficulties. If you suddenly inherit a million dollars and go to Europe, you are going to bring along your bad temper, your childish ways, and your capacity to hate. Nothing will change because we react without choice. We think we know ourselves. We believe that we are good, intelligent, and pretty much in control, but we are like machines driven by the stimulus-response activity of life.

If we observe ourselves honestly, we see that we have no choices. Life takes our energy, robs us of our life-force. We don't do anything but are done to! Awakening means that things that once made us angry no longer have that power over us. We have developed a sense of relativity and perspective. Awakening is an increase of consciousness, finding meaning to life beyond the daily grind. With a greater understanding of who we are, we no longer blame others or life or God for our problems, but face them in ourselves knowing that it is we who must change. The Christ asks us: "Why do you see the speck in your brother's eye but do not notice the log that is in yours?" Awakening from sleep is a liberation from these continual responses to life over which we have no control. It allows us to begin to understand what Christ meant by the "kingdom of heaven." The kingdom of

God is not external or visible. It is a spiritual idea. We are explicitly told that it is not of this world. Like so many of the sayings of Christ, the "kingdom of heaven" has vast meaning. In our usual state of little attention and sleep, we see only the tip of the iceberg and miss the great mass that is beneath.

The kingdom of heaven is not a place, not ahead of us in time but present within us as a possible state of being. It is of a spiritual nature. Theologians have distorted its meaning by connecting it with paradise, something unattainable for us until after this life. But Christ spoke of a kingdom here on earth, attainable by each of us. He says: "Truly, I say to you, there are some standing here who will not taste death before they see the Son of Man coming in his kingdom."

The usual interpretation has been that this is a reference to the Second Coming. But then the disciples died. There had been no Second Coming and the people didn't know what to do with this saying of Christ. Yet Christ was stating that while we are alive we can know the kingdom of heaven. And he tells us how to do it. We find repeated seventeen times in the New Testament that only those who have ears can hear, that is, only those who have awakened can understand. In the Gospel of John we read: "Why do you not understand what I say? It is because you cannot bear to hear my word. He who is of God hears the word of God. The reason that you do not hear, then, is that you are not of God." The term "not of God" refers to a person not awakened to sacred reality. For when we live in sleep, completely drowned in ourselves, we cannot be aware of the divine character of reality.

THE STAGES

In the *Book of Isaiah*, we are given the witness of a human being's awakening to his spiritual reality. There are three stages to the seeker's vision. First, the discovery and experience of the divine: "I saw the Lord sitting upon a throne, high up and lifted." Surely all of us have had one moment in our lives when something broke through to us, whether through joy, suffering, or beauty. This is a moment of tasting the sacredness of life.

Isaiah shows us what happens in such a moment: "Woe is me, for I am a man of unclean lips." When the awareness of the holy touches us, we cannot but feel shame and remorse for our disregard of the sacred and our subsequent inappropriate relationship to life. That is where the message of Christ comes in, so full of hope and empowerment because it is through remorse that we find mercy and forgiveness. The gratitude we feel for this unmerited mercy enables us to begin again. That is the starting point, where we can begin to trust in divine grace instead of in our own illusions, where we can begin to live a life of humility and thanksgiving oriented toward God.

The third stage is the realization that our Creator gives us the power to say yes or no to the divine call. This alone shows God's love for us. We are given a choice: "Who will go for us?" Isaiah's vision provides a key to understanding the process of awakening. When we are asked "who will go for God," it is not a matter of going off to distant places or of enduring terrible suffering, but of offering our life to the Holy through acceptance and compassion. Our lives are to be transformed into a God-centered existence. It is not so much a matter of *what* we do, but of *who* we are. For religion is a way of living, not a thing that we believe in. When it is merely a belief, it is external to our lives and all spiritual teachers condemn it, speaking of people who "honor me with their lips while their hearts are far from me."

We must change, which means going against the current of our ingrained habits and attitudes. But just as the Spirit urges us to seek, so does It assist us in finding. These words of Christ are for each one of us: "Fear not, for it is your Father's good pleasure to give you the kingdom."

We cannot remain as we are if we wish to experience life in such a way that we "enter the kingdom of heaven" here and now. Some of the most intense teachings of Christ are found in the Beatitudes. There we are told: "Blessed are the poor in spirit, for theirs is the kingdom of heaven." What is meant by the "poor in spirit"? Surely, Jesus does not mean the weak in spirit or the financially destitute. For it is not external poverty, but humility that is the key to spiritual evolution. He is referring to those who are no longer victims of the sleep of pride, who have been released from their illusions about themselves. They have emptied themselves so that they may be filled with God. This process of emptying that is found throughout the great religious teachings is a journey, and more than that, it is a search.

THE SEARCH

Have you ever asked yourself after a long, frustrating day: Why am I doing this? Isn't there more to life? Michelangelo asked this question. And this was his answer at the end of his life: "Painting and sculpture have ruined me. It would have been better if in my youth I had hired myself out to make sulfur matches. I regret that I have not done enough for the salvation of my soul."

Here was a man who gave outstanding works of art to humanity. They will be studied and admired till the end of time. And yet, he died in despair, for in drawing all those sketches, chiseling all that marble, and endlessly mixing his paints, he had omitted to give his attention to the fundamental questions. Even though they were the very subject matter of his work, he did not apply them to himself. He did not ask until it was too late. He did not seek beyond his art. He did not find that for which his soul was truly yearning.

One of the great tragedies of our time is that our technology, with all of its advantages and advances, has not helped us to deal with the meaning of life. In fact, it has done the opposite. It has dehumanized our lives, brought new pressures upon us, placed us on tight time schedules, and turned us into cogs in the machinery of society. Our daily lives have become treadmills. We have created specialists and computers that take care of all our needs. Our scientists with all their amazing equipment look out into the universe and see harmony and order, but do not see the presence of a unifying power and intelligence. Yet Carl Sagan tells us that we are all "star stuff." We are all made of the matter and energy that permeates the universe. Nevertheless, many scientists do not equate this oneness with the revelations of the great religions.

The more scientific knowledge grows, the more it reveals this mystery of the inherent unity of all things. One of the latest insights in physics is known as the "unified theory" which seeks to prove that all people, all ecosystems, all animals, all creation issue from one source. Meanwhile, movies, television, and education teach us to get ahead in the world, to pay the rent, to be on time, to do as others do, to look out for number one. The Russian philosopher P. D. Ouspensky observed: "It is only when you realize that life is leading you nowhere that it begins to have meaning." When we no longer follow the enforced priorities of our society, we begin to uncover the real issues.

Even religious institutions often do not know these questions. In my years in seminary, I saw people on the verge of nervous breakdowns, and in a constant frenzy generated by the absurd demands of academia. There was no time for prayer, no time for God. There was plenty of talk about God, plenty of tests on what people thought about God, but there was no time for encountering God. Why? Because very few persons were practicing the way of inner transformation depicted by Christ. No one asked the right questions, those that rise out of the core of our being. External religion has replaced this life-giving asking with rules to follow, because rules become easy answers. Some teachings insist that women wear hats or veils in places of worship. The question "is this necessary for the salvation of the soul, for knowing God?" is not even brought up.

The apostle Paul tells us to "test everything," like the money-changers of old who bit into the coin to see if it was real. We need to find out what is true and what is not through our heart and conscience, for that is where the Spirit communicates with us. But it is necessary to use more than the mind in order to understand. We cannot simply say "if I can't see it, it's not real," because God is spirit and it is in spirit that we experience the spiritual Presence. All of life is rooted in spirit.

THE GOAL

One of the great breakthroughs on the spiritual journey is the discovery that everything we are seeking is within us. Certainly, there are books to be read, knowledge to be acquired, teachers to be heard. But eventually we must turn within and encounter the inner Master.

This inner Master has been called our Higher Self, the still, small voice, the Holy Spirit and many other names. The fact is that the eternal Presence that we seek can only be found face to face in an intimate spiritual experience. The Scriptures tell us that the Christ knocks at the door of our hearts and that all we need to do is to open it. These metaphors are all centered on the idea voiced by Jeremiah that consciousness of God is "written in our hearts."

However, there is a great paradox to be dealt with before entering this realm. We can only have such an encounter by transcending our ego and thereby becoming receptive to the divine activity within. We have to get out of the way so that we can find ourselves.

The inner life cannot blossom unless we have minimized the dominance of that egotistic power which claims to be our identity but is actually entirely fraudulent.

DANGEROUS PATHS

On my journey in search of meaning, I had the good fortune to come across a very special community. It was actually a school, an esoteric school, where people studied the teachings of G. I. Gurdjieff.

The students came from all walks of life, all socio-economic levels and educational backgrounds. We had one thing in common: a burning desire for inner development or spiritual awakening. Most of us had been seeking knowledge of a specific kind for years. Some had traveled as far as Tibet and India. There was a story of two students who became disciples of a Tibetan holy man who, after some time, told them to go back to America to find a teaching that would give them enlightenment. He then gave them a latitude and longitude that turned out to be the spot in northern California where this school was founded.

As with other such communities, our school had a teacher. This person was said to be a "conscious being," that is, someone whose inner efforts had led him into higher levels of awareness. He was certainly different from most anyone you are likely to meet. His gaze pierced right to the marrow of my being and left me helplessly exposed in all my imperfections. He was a man who radiated a strange blend of rare gentleness and inner strength.

Most important of all, we were held together by the ideas of the Gurdjieff system. Culled from ancient teachings and presented in incredibly pragmatic ways, these methods of inner transformation make possible genuine change. There was no question here of some vague faith in a spiritual promised land or future state of bliss. The "Work" as it is called demands personal verification and provides the psychological tools for immediate application to one's attitudes.

Members of this community made tremendous sacrifices. We lived in "teaching houses," where part of the instruction was to learn to put up with each other. There were weekly meetings and daily chores that forced the body to submit itself to one's higher aims. There were also demands for regular payments that were sometimes exorbitant. The money kept the community running, a community that had teaching houses in many cities and was becoming international. But we believed that the real reason for the financial pressure was aimed at insuring an individual's commitment to the task of personal development.

We didn't clearly understand that "payment" for the sake of spiritual results can never be an external activity. Real payment is internal effort against one's selfishness and pride. The money used in this kind of payment is made of effort and intentional suffering in order to break through toward a new level of understanding and behavior.

With all these requirements, you may be surprised to

know that the first two years in this environment were extraordinarily blissful. In this subculture disconnected from dull materialism and relentless advertising, we were given rare opportunities to rediscover our essential nature beneath the facades of personality. We learned to free ourselves from the unnecessary anger and irritation that poison so many lives. We marveled at the depth of the human potential as revealed by the best minds of civilized humanity: Pythagoras, Plato, Epictetus, Goethe, Blake, and many more. The purpose of this school was not only to lead us toward inner development, but also to gather and preserve the works created by the more illumined minds from all times and places. To live in such an environment in itself contributed to transformation.

We were not merely gathered to study ideas of common interest. It was a matter of life and death for many of us. We were prepared to sacrifice everything—ambition, family, comfort—in order to find regenerating truth. Many of us were baby boomers who had survived the sixties, wandered the continents throughout the seventies, and refused to become self-satisfied yuppies of the eighties and nineties.

Becoming free of psychological baggage of the past, and uncovering new vistas of understanding is worth all the money and electronic gadgets the world has to offer. Individually, we encountered that wonder toward life so important to the teachings of Socrates; that will so fundamental to all esoteric methods; and that universal goodness revealed at the heart of all religions.

Here was a community of people in the process of being

purified of their petty selfishness. Here were people with a new dignity and control over their irrational impulses and unpleasant manifestations. What could be better for the health and welfare of any community? A common goal, a common sacrifice, a common understanding: surely, these are the foundations of any long lasting gathering of people.

And yet, certain very mundane conflicts began to surface among us. Who was closest to the teacher? Who had been around the longest? Who would give orders? The power inherent in the ideas had altered the course of our lives, but they were insufficient to overcome that all too familiar egotism.

In analyzing this discrepancy between the knowledge of human transformation available to us and the increasingly absurd conflicts found in any group situation, I noticed the following factors:

1) The organization had become more important than the ideas that founded it.

2) The lifestyle of effort and sacrifice that we willingly entered into was now a dogmatic requirement rather than a personal commitment.

3) Students who had once searched for higher consciousness with pure motives were now satisfied with positions of authority within the little society they had created.

4) The teacher who was once at the center of activities now retired to a lofty, inaccessible position surrounded by a protective entourage.

5) The demands for money began to translate into luxurious possessions for the leadership rather than practical needs for the community.

6) The ideas themselves were reduced to learning by rote rather than used in dynamic application. A robot-like atmosphere was created as people offered memorized platitudes and imitated personalities rather than insights born from the furnace of intimate experience.

Finally, I came to the conclusion that it was necessary for me to leave. If I was to think for myself, which the teaching insisted upon, then I had to follow my intuitions rather than the dictates of the group. It became increasingly difficult to put up with the concept that if one left the school, all was lost. So nearly four years after finding a family of fellow seekers the like of which I had never hoped to discover, I left quietly to start again on my own. It was an experience as shattering as any divorce or loss of a loved one. But I soon learned that the best thing that had happened to me after joining that community was the act of leaving it.

I discovered that when I payed the price to renounce my will for a higher purpose, and then payed an even greater one to take it back in order to be true to myself, a learning occurs that can be acquired in no other way and will always be a part of me.

The community changed the course of my life. It introduced me to myself in a way that I could not have done on my own. It sustained me in making efforts that were sometimes beyond my natural capacity to endure. And it taught me to know when I had to listen to the inner master alone over anyone else, however apparently enlightened they may seem.

We often assume that we already possess this power. But it is generally nothing more than the self-will that has dominated us since infancy. The process is the same in nearly all the great teachings of humanity, from the mystery schools of Egypt and Greece to modern esoteric organizations seeking higher consciousness. The inner journey is a cyclical spiral woven in paradox. We lose ourselves in order to find ourselves; we join a community to develop our individuality; we leave the group to work for the good of that larger group named humanity.

NEW FORMS

In 1922, Gurdjieff, one of the great masters of all time, created a community outside of Paris that he called *The Institute for the Harmonious Development of Man*. Ten years later, he disbanded the group and presented his teachings in a new form. He had done this several times before. He also forced his long-time students to leave him and reconstitute the Work on their own. This suggests, among other things, that communities have a specific lifespan and tend to crystallize within a short time. Individuals must rediscover the teachings for themselves and recreate the forms in which they are lived out. There are forms all around us that have long outlived their original aim. Like everything else, communities must die and be reborn to remain true to their purpose.

The greatest danger perhaps is that "higher consciousness" is experienced as some cold, detached relationship to oneself and to the world. In the school of which I was a student, our "conscious teacher" was certainly a man who had liberated himself from personality through extensive work on himself and who had deep perception into the psychology of other people. Yet he was heard telling one of his students that the man's daughter was nothing more than a "ragdoll" since she was a stimulus-response machine without the light of evolved consciousness. More importantly, the unabashed veneration in which he was held by his students turned him into a king and his followers into sheep. There was also a mercilessness toward the needs of individuals who were part of this School, let alone outside persons whom they referred to as "life people." These sometimes vicious attitudes were all sanctified by distortions of the teachings. Clearly, esoteric paths are not meant to lead us toward a rejection of all that is human, but toward a transfiguration of life so that, as human beings, we can become channels of Divine Love.

Sometimes we learn to undertake the inner journey when our lives are shattered by painful blows and we become aware of a deeper reality. Sometimes a great joy brings new light into our daily routine. Then our rationally organized, mutually agreed upon reality breaks down. That is when the possibility of something real is born, for nothing new can enter the old wineskins of a self-satisfied existence. It is in those disruptive moments when we have lost our self-confidence, when we have lost our false sense of security that we begin to ask the really important questions, those that only a transcendent, yet immanent power can answer: Who am I? What am I meant to do in this short life? What is life for? What is death?

Each of us can find answers to the deepest questions of our souls. They have been written in our hearts precisely so that we may turn within and ask, and in doing so, come face to face with our true natures.

CLEANSING THE CUP

Our era is one of synthesizing universal spiritual teachings so that they may be applied to our daily existence. In this context, disciplines are useful, but the only true discipline is that of being present to the passing moment. We must begin where we are, in the "here and now." Those familiar with eastern spiritual literature know that this is a fundamental insight of great value. The present moment which we take for granted is none other than the intersection of the finite and the infinite. The key issue is: how do we access these depths? How do we break out of the haze which keeps us on the familiar treadmill of our countless anxieties?

In the teachings of Socrates, with his call to "know thyself," in the sayings of Christ, and in the psychological system put together by Gurdjieff, we find not only a map but an obligation to roll up our sleeves and undertake a journey. We must travel through our inner jungles, seeking the divine light at the center of our being.

But something hinders us on the journey. This part of us is the outer self, that which will disappear into nothingness when our time is up. Like a cloud blocking the sun, the false self hides our true nature and turns us into individuals whose happiness is based on what others think of us. This artificial self demands an audience, wants praise, and keeps a record of those who do not acknowledge it. In that condition, happiness cannot be genuine since it depends on others and needs continual stimulation. This false self cannot seek out greater awareness with such constant distraction.

We are preoccupied with making good impressions, and keeping up appearances. We are, according to Maurice Nicoll, like people always standing on their toes who do not understand why they are exhausted. For this false self exhausts us by forcing us to strain to be what we are not. If we were not dominated by this usurper, most of our anxiety and nervousness would vanish. Our relationship with ourselves and with others would change. But this false self never admits anything and loves only itself. It keeps us from discovering who we truly are.

This false self arises in us through unconscious imitation of our parents, from following what our culture dictates that we ought to be, and from imagining what we think we should be. This surface self is also engendered by vanity which stands in the way of any real spiritual development. Vanity comes from the Latin word *vanitas* which means emptiness. The dictionary defines it as a "state destitute of reality." Like Narcissus captivated by his reflection in the pool, our lives become centered on ourselves and we lose sight of the purpose and meaning of life. We find importance in our separateness whereas our only true value is in becoming part of a greater whole. Vanity's separateness is death indeed since we cut ourselves off from the roots of existence.

Unless we are liberated from vanity, it has full power over us. The consciousness of transcendent reality cannot take root in the superficial part of ourselves.

THE CREATION OF THE FALSE SELF

As with many others, my teen years were spent in a blur of twisted values. In my case, they were reinforced by wrestling coaches who were bent on creating violent and emotionally damaged creatures in four short years. Under the banner of such revered philosophies as "when the going gets tough, the tough get going," or "we're number one," the gym room became a more powerful chamber of transformation than the sanctuary. The worship of winning and of the "team spirit" completely overran whatever sensitivities had taken root within many of the young men.

Some high school coaches seem devoted to the annihilation of any real feeling in the teenage boys under their control. They mold their minds through humiliation and tyranny, forcing them to become members of that male fellowship bent on power and dominance, a fellowship that causes and fights wars in all centuries. Innocence and gentleness are crushed under the rules of brute force and hatred of the adversary. The wrestling mat is a terrible rite of passage as effective as any tribal ritual. It is the same with many other sports: winning is everything, losing is disgraceful.

I have witnessed coaches turn into foaming beasts in the locker rooms as they roar at players who can only bow their heads in shame. Shame is in fact the coaches' secret weapon, much like the boot-camp trick of breaking down a person until nothing is left but a psychopathic killing machine. The child within is then buried alive.

As with the wolf packs of the wild, it is all a matter of raw survival: the loner gets eaten, the crippled are abandoned. And nearly everything and everyone conspires to sustain the power of the pack. Movies and media depict the currently acceptable definition of man or woman; teachers often spoon-feed the culture's priorities and values to their students; sports direct the flow of young people straight into the prefabricated molds approved by society; and burgeoning sexual energy provides the electricity that keeps everyone moving through the assembly line.

In many cases movie stars represent archetypes of socially-sanctioned roles. Silvester Stallone or Clint Eastwood can stamp a whole generation with a set of values that they will take to the grave. John Wayne paved the way for thousands of volunteers who grew up on his bravado to the rice paddies and jungles of Viet Nam. Goebbels himself, Hitler's propaganda minister, would be impressed with the mind control perpetrated by Hollywood's fantasies flickering on the silver screen, not to mention the countless video stores invading every neighborhood. The mass media's incestuous feeding on itself has created a vicious cycle in which it is hard to tell who created whom. Does Madison Avenue merely reflect our desires or does it stimulate them with its endless barrage of images flashing before our eyes?

Our work is to get rid of their false view of reality, to clean out what stands in the way of receiving the divine Presence. But cleaning the outside does not do the job. It is all a matter of inner effort for that is what will properly motivate outward behavior. What keeps us from receiving God? More than anything else, it is that within us which is expressed in all forms of violence, anger, depression, cynicism, doubt. It is from these negative emotions that we must cleanse ourselves, from always thinking unpleasant things about others and finding fault. We have a right not to live in this way. But we must first of all recognize that these are habits over which we have no control. We need to reach a point where we no longer receive pleasure by indulging in these destructive feelings and recognize that they are contagious, infecting everyone around us. We must have the courage to go beyond our self-justification.

GIVING AND RECEIVING

How then are we to interact with the people and circumstances we encounter in daily life? We have all heard the biblical saying "it is better to give than to receive." Since these words are considered those of the Christ, everyone generally assumes that they are golden wisdom. While it is true that giving as an act of compassion and generosity is critical to any genuine maturity of spirit, there is also another side to the coin.

In an age of radical individualism, where independence is prized over most everything else, there are many persons who are virtually incapable of the act of receiving. You know the type, and maybe you are the type who says proudly and defiantly: "I can do it on my own"; "I don't need any help"; "leave me alone"; "I'd rather starve than take a hand-out." These attitudes are sanctioned by the American myth of rugged individualism.

Some of these qualities are laudable. But consider this behavior from the perspective of the interconnection of all existence. Our western culture praises accomplishment and the acts of *doing* and *acquiring*. It generally rejects or disdains the eastern approach that values the more contemplative lifestyle of *being*. The pace of our society often forces most of us to live each day at frantic speed. Many of us are driven by economic necessity, unbounded ambition, or an insatiable appetite for new gadgets. The very nature of our environment supports the *survival of the fittest* level of existence that is utterly dehumanizing.

At the same time, becoming receptive as a mode of living is central to all spiritual traditions. We have nothing to give until we have received some degree of inspiration. We can therefore conclude that in order to give we must be able to receive. It is not one or the other, for they enable and sustain each other. When we refuse to receive—whether love, charity, or counsel—we isolate ourselves at our spiritual peril. The humility of receiving is the fertile soil out of which arises the wisdom of giving.

Spiritual masters have revealed to us what is perhaps the most powerful form of giving. In every century, we find stories of seekers going to a teacher for new understanding.

The most highly prized and intimate communication is shared in silence. The master and disciple sit together in a common receptive mode, generally that of meditation. A mysterious "giving" occurs that would not be received otherwise. The gift from master to student is a receptivity that calls forth a giving from the source that gave both of them life. The Teacher who told us that it is better to give than to receive also said: "Without me you can do nothing." In other words: "You have to receive before you can give."

We are all receivers in need of air, food, and love. But we also have another need, and that is to give of ourselves. This is the cyclic movement of existence itself.

We are materializations of a giving and receiving that are two movements of the same activity. We have received everything as a gift, beginning with this wondrous phenomenon called life, which after a few decades must be given back. This is not a tragedy but rather an experience of ecstasy. To go gracefully with the flow of giving and receiving requires trust and acceptance. These two key words, so full of implications, are the cornerstones of spiritual teachings. They are also interchangeable synonyms of giving and receiving. To give is to trust that the gift will be received. To receive is to accept what is given. We can take this a step further and compare this movement to the act of breathing. We give when we exhale and receive when we inhale. Then we find that every instant of our existence is governed by giving and receiving. To stop giving or receiving is to die. This is a physical truth as well as a psychological and spiritual one.

When we enter wholly and joyfully into the great cosmic movement that blesses the universe with life in every moment, we discover our own ultimate fulfillment.

We can hide from ourselves, but we cannot hide from the ever present source of our being. And it takes the courage of radical effort to face the truth about ourselves. Only then can we realize that just as a child needs our love the most when he or she deserves it the least, so does Divine Unconditional Love give us mercy and forgiveness in spite of ourselves. Only then can we realize that it is not we who are seeking God but God who is seeking us. Our job is to make ourselves receptive to the ineffable Love trying to reach us. Prayer and meditation are meant to open us to God so that we may be infused by this healing and transforming consciousness. This reception makes us channels of grace. We are ultimately capable of incarnating Divine Love. For the spiritual dimension is not out there somewhere, but works in and through us.

The teaching of Jesus deals with the inner quality of life in the individual. Genuine service can only come from there. Continual alignment with our deeper forces brings peace, relaxation and silence into our mind and heart so that we may become receptive.

Leo Tolstoy gave up his aristocratic life to live in such universal consciousness. He expressed his experience of spiritual reality in this way: "One knows God not so much through reason or even through the heart, but through one's feelings of complete dependence on Him, akin to the feelings experienced by an unweaned child in the arms of its mother. It does not know who holds it, warms and feeds it, but it knows that there is this someone, and more than merely knows, it loves that being."

However difficult the struggle may be, we have help. One of the great fathers of the church tells us that if we desire the Holy Spirit with our whole heart, we have already received it. There is a story that Socrates told long ago and it has been repeated in many different philosophies. A seeker of truth went to a great master looking for knowledge and understanding. The holy man took him down to a lake and suddenly pushed his head under water and held him there. The young man began to kick and become frantic. Right at the moment of drowning, the old sage lifted him up. As the youth breathed in the life-giving air, the wise man told him: "When you want understanding as much as you wanted to breathe, then you will find it."

The next chapter introduces two specific methods for practical transformation, followed by spiritual counsels taken from the Christian spiritual tradition.

VII

Approaches to Spiritual Awakening

The previous chapters have suggested that religion—and Christianity in particular—has as sole purpose the metamorphosis of human beings from two-legged animals with an intellect into caring members of the universe conscious of their significance and obligations. I will now present practical methods that can lead to the fulfillment of these possibilities.

While it is true that the Bible does not provide a blueprint to spiritual development or a specific list of exercises, a number of traditions have appeared through the centuries to assist those who sought for such evolution. Many of these venerable systems are time-tested and still valid for today while others were meant for a certain time and place and are now outdated.

I will present two specific "methodologies" that are informed by both ancient and contemporary insights on the human potential. Both methods understand Christianity as a path of transformation. Their approaches to inner work on oneself are founded on pragmatic and verifiable human experience that, with long and intensive effort, leads to new becoming. Our first encounter is with an esoteric system of thought and exercises known as the Fourth Way developed by Gurdjieff. The second teaching comes from the German spiritual master Karlfried Graf Dürckheim.

Though the teachings of the two men are not directly related and they did not know each other, it is easy to find strong parallels between them. One striking example is Dürckheim's concept of critical watchfulness and Gurdjieff's method of self-observation. Both ideas are rooted in the ancient Christian method of *nepsis* (watch of the heart) and are comparable to key ideas of other traditions, such as Buddhism's mindfulness.

My own spiritual journey is indebted to these individuals in very specific ways. They came into my life at critical junctures and changed the direction and purpose of my existence. Though I was ultimately brought back into Christianity through the writings of Thomas Merton and the teachings of the Philokalia, the latter ideas would not have resonated in me as deeply and pragmatically without the foundation I acquired through studying Gurdjieff's methods.

THE FOURTH WAY: A METHOD OF TRANSFORMATION

In the 1927 manuscript *Introduction to Fragments of an Unknown Teaching*, P. D. Ouspensky, a key teacher of the Fourth Way, wrote:

The predominant emotion in me was fear—fear to lose

myself, fear to disappear in something unknown . . . I remember a phrase in a letter I wrote at that time: "I am writing this letter to you, but who will write the next letter, signing it with my name, and what he will say I do not know." This was the fear.(1)

Ouspensky, a Russian philosopher, was referring to the transformative impact of what is called the "System," the "Work," or the "Fourth Way." This teaching is a method of intense personal effort performed on oneself for the purpose of knowing oneself objectively and evolving into a higher state of consciousness that awakens us to a whole new experience of reality.

George Ivanovitch Gurdjieff brought these powerful ideas to the West from ancient and secret sources in the East. This extraordinary system of thought ranges from the most intimate, psychological insights to a grandiose cosmology linking the individual with the universe. It is a synthesis of practices and teachings formatted for the western scientific mind. It is named the Fourth Way to differentiate it from the other ways of conscious evolution: the Way of the Monk, the Way of the Fakir, the Way of the Yogi. Each of these classic methods of human transformation focus on different aspects of the individual: emotional, physical, intellectual. The Fourth Way deals with all of these dimensions at once, seeking to create a balanced individual whose inner work of transformation occurs in the midst of his or her daily activities. It is not necessary to live in monasteries or ashrams in order to apply this spiritual concentration. Yet the efforts made are as intense and demanding as any of the practices that take place in those settings. The Work is entirely inner, invisible, and individual.

The evolution of human consciousness is a matter of personal efforts and is therefore a rare exception among the majority of human beings. To those who would wonder at the seeming unfairness of this assertion, Ouspensky responds that most people simply do not want to awaken. To become a different being, we must want it greatly and over many years. Without the necessary efforts we will not evolve. Moreover, we must acquire qualities that we believe we already possess but in fact do not. In the Fourth Way, this insight is the first step in the direction of inner evolution: we do not know ourselves.

Man has invented many machines, and he knows that a complicated machine needs sometimes years of careful study before one can use it or control it. But he does not apply this knowledge to himself, although he himself is a much more complicated machine than any machine he has invented. (2)

This "machine" is brought into motion by external influences. All actions, ideas, and emotions are responses to the stimulus of external events. For Gurdjieff, such mechanical persons are asleep to their true condition and virtually incapable of change. "By himself, he is just an automaton with a certain store of memories of previous experiences, and a certain amount of reserve energy."(3)

Human beings, therefore, cannot "do." Everything happens to us as to puppets pulled by invisible strings.

Ouspensky believed that if we could perceive this phenomenon, then things would begin to change for us. We human beings are not merely stimulus-response machines, but machines that can know that we are machines! Realizing this, we may find ways to cease being simply reactive organisms.

THE ILLUSION OF UNITY

Another central idea in the Fourth Way is that the individual is not one. We have no permanent I or Ego. Every thought, feeling, sensation, desire is an I which believes that it is the whole person. Yet none of these I's are connected and each depends on the change of external circumstances. To make matters worse, there are often impenetrable defenses between each I which the Work calls "buffers" separating these sub-personalities from one another.

Gurdjieff stated that one of our most important mistakes is our illusion about our unity.

His I changes as quickly as his thoughts, feelings, and moods, and he makes the profound mistake in considering himself always one and the same person; in reality he is always a different person, not the one he was a moment ago. (4)

Our every thought and desire lives separately and independently from the whole. According to Gurdjieff, we are made of thousands of separate I's, often unknown to one another, and sometime mutually exclusive and hostile to each other. "Man is a plurality. Man's name is legion." (5) The alternation of I's is controlled by accidental external influences. There is nothing in us able to control the change of I's, mainly because we do not notice it. Each separate I calls itself I and acts in the name of the whole person. This explains why people so often make decisions and so seldom carry them out. A little self-observation will prove that we usually think, feel, move and respond without our being aware of what is happening within us.

This self-observation is in fact the first practical effort required in the Fourth Way. The student is to create an "observing I" which observes with objectivity his or her inner activity. To develop an objective space within, which can see without judging, is extremely difficult but is also the first breakthrough out of our mechanical behavior and the state of sleep in which it keeps us.

STATES OF CONSCIOUSNESS

Consciousness is a particular kind of awareness concerning who we are, where we are in the moment, and what we know in the deepest dimension of our being. It never remains the same but can be made continuous and controllable through special efforts and study.

The Fourth Way points to four states of consciousness: sleep, waking state, self-consciousness, and objective consciousness. Most everyone lives only in the first two states. The third state, self-consciousness, is one that we believe we possess even though we are conscious of ourselves only in rare flashes. Such flashes come in exceptional moments, in highly emotional states, in times of danger, or in new and unexpected circumstances. We have no control over their coming and going.

> If we knew the quantity of wrong observations, wrong theories, wrong deductions and conclusions made in this state (our ordinary consciousness), we should cease to believe ourselves altogether. (6)

Dr. Kathleen Speeth, in her book *The Gurdjieff Work*, observes that anyone who has a difficult time accepting the notion that as we are we have but few moments of true self-consciousness, ought to make a study of the loose jaws and vacant stares of people in public places and in situations where they do not think that they are being observed.

According to the Fourth Way, the central obstacle to higher levels of consciousness is a phenomenon known as *identification*. Ouspensky described it in this manner:

> In this state man has no separate awareness. He is lost in whatever he happens to be doing, feeling, thinking. Because he is lost, immersed, not present to himself, this condition is known as a state of waking sleep. (7)

When we are identified, our attention is directed outward and we are lost to ourselves. Self-consciousness is then a state in which we become aware of ourselves and are no longer hypnotized by the external event before us. There is a higher level still to be reached which the Work calls "objective consciousness." In this state, we come into contact with the real world from which we are seemingly cut off.

ESSENCE AND PERSONALITY

In order to see clearly the roots of our psychological distortions, the Fourth Way defines two aspects of the individual: essence and personality. Essence is what a person is born with, personality is that which is acquired. All that is learned, both unconsciously through imitation, and through acquired likes and dislikes, constitutes the outer part of the person, that which is changed by outer circumstances. Though personality is necessary, it must not be left to dominate essence or it will produce artificial persons cut off from their true natures.

> This means that with a quick and early growth of personality, growth of essence can practically stop at a very early age, and as a result we see men and women externally quite grown up, but whose essence remains at the age of ten or twelve. (8)

According to Rodney Collin, one of Ouspensky's primary students who started his own Fourth Way School in Mexico, the fundamental abnormality in human beings lies precisely in the divergence between personality and essence. The more nearly we know ourselves for what we are, the more we approach wisdom. The more our imagination about ourselves diverges from what we actually are, the more insane we become.

> Unless a man first finds himself, finds his own essential nature and destiny, and begins from them, all his efforts and achievements will be built only on the sand of personality, and at the first serious shock the whole

structure will crumble, perhaps destroying him in its fall.(9)

Through the practice of "self-remembering," we can separate ourselves from the pretenses and imitations that have enslaved us since childhood and return to who we actually are. Such a return to our essential nature is accompanied by a sense of liberation unlike any other. "To thyself be true" is the first commandment on the way of self-development.

SELF-REMEMBERING

Maurice Nicoll states in his *Psychological Commentaries on the Teachings of Gurdjieff and Ouspensky* that as you make progress in the Work, "what you took as yourself begins to look like a little prison-house far away in the valley beneath you."(10)

This is a vivid expression of the "third state of consciousness" or "self-remembering" as it is called. These flashes of greater consciousness are the unexpected results of the strenuous efforts made in order not to lose oneself in the rush of outer circumstances, to be cleansed from the acids of negativity, and to maintain a heightened awareness grounded in the present.

The student is to reach a point where he or she can make the choice not to react automatically to external stimuli. This requires going against the grain, resisting long established habits and self-indulgences. The question is as basic as: can you find the willpower to choose not to react angrily to something that makes you angry? Rather than being wasted in such an outburst, the energy accumulated through this effort can be available for a moment of intensified consciousness. This moment will flood you with peace or quiet joy or a sense of profound liberation. Oddly enough, these rare and precious moments often come in very paradoxical events. When night is darkest, a shaft of light can suddenly break through. Self-remembering, combined with the insights of objective self-observation, assists in the creation of a balanced individual who is not completely under the sway of his or her inborn nature and acquired habits. It is not possible to experience a vaster sense of reality if we are entirely under the dominance of the intellect to the exclusion of the emotional or the instinctive part of our nature and vice-versa. In attempting to make the machine work right, it is necessary to change attitudes and behavior developed over years of wrong functioning.

Maurice Nicoll gives a hint of these first stages of real change in his *Psychological Commentaries:*

This gradual withdrawal of energy from the customary, easily resentful and brittle feeling of 'I' is accompanied by a gradual new and broader feeling of I, as if one were living in a larger place . . . It is like being introduced to a new civilization, to another form of life. (11)

He points out that by using the inner camera of self-observation, we begin to open a mind above the level of the sensual mind. Here is where the psychological experiences of the Fourth Way begin to reveal their numinous and "religious" character.

Self-remembering, then, is a process of being lifted out of our ordinary sense of self into a purified, detached space well known to those long practiced in meditation. But in the Fourth Way this birth of new awareness can be accomplished while one crosses a city street or takes out the trash. Nevertheless, despite the practical approach of the Work, self-remembering remains as intangible and paradoxical as any spiritual exercise. Reminiscent of the Zen koan, Rodney Collin told his students that we cannot remember ourselves until we forget ourselves. And at the height of his powers of understanding, he united the Fourth Way with the wisdom of all times and places: "To feel beauty, to feel truth, that is self-remembering. Self-remembering is the awareness of the presence of God."(12)

The idea that we are not awake but live in a partial dream state from which we can awaken opens radically new horizons. The illusions we foster concerning ourselves melt under the light of increased consciousness and we awaken to new dimensions of reality that set us free. We are then able to relate to the world around us without the usual defenses, masks, and confusion that constitute much of human interaction. We become capable of a new kind of compassion.

At their core, the originators of the Fourth Way as we know it today were religious men in the true sense of the term. Work on oneself leads to a liberation that can be compared to the enlightenment and divinization of more traditionally religious methods.

DIVIDED ATTENTION

One of the central teachings in ancient religious orders was the intentional division of attention between oneself and the outside world. By splitting our attention in two directions, we learn to be aware of ourselves acting, feeling or thinking in relation to the outer world. This is how the Fourth Way teaches us to "remember ourselves," by moments at first and then with increasing frequency. In proportion as we learn to remember ourselves, our actions acquire a consistency that is impossible as long as our attention is locked in one direction. Divided attention is the chief characteristic of self-remembering. There are certain experiences in which this takes place naturally, such as the sensations of love where an intense awareness of oneself and of another occurs at the same time. This is a foretaste of the next stage of consciousness.

A certain stage of relaxation is helpful in dividing one's attention. When I am able to divide my attention between the outside world and awareness of myself, I can see my reactions to ideas and events without being instantly victimized by my response to the particular stimulus. This in turn allows me to remain in a state of serenity that generates feelings of healing and liberation.

Due to the power of the Work and the impact it can have on the psyche, it is possible to let oneself become enslaved to a teacher or an organization. Yet the Fourth Way is precisely meant to avoid all that. It is meant to lead us to our true Master, the Master within, and to transcend even the Work's own magnificent thought structures so that every student can find for himself or herself a higher consciousness that constantly seeks to reach us if only we would make the effort to awaken and ready ourselves to receive its treasures of wisdom and regeneration.

THE NEXT STAGE

After my seminary years and encounter with the great visionaries of Christianity, I was better able to understand why Gurdjieff spoke of his teachings as esoteric Christianity. Once again, I must emphasize that the word esoteric was originally understood as "inner" rather than "hidden." It is not a matter of robed individuals meeting in secret chambers, but of teachings dealing with spiritual evolution.

The Gurdjieff work leaves off, in my mind, where Christian mysticism begins. The methods it teaches are necessary because of the wrong working of our psychological make-up and the distorting impact of education and of our culture. Christian mysticism is the next step. Gurdjieff rarely spoke of God, and let his students discover that mystery for themselves through verifiable means rather than through "faith" (understood as mere belief).

The roundabout way of my re-entry into Christianity was necessary for me because true teachings are virtually impossible to find in institutional religions. More importantly, a vision of universal truth is critical for our era, one that requires the accumulation of knowledge resulting from personal effort and sacrifice. Few schools or teachers are making these connections. Moreover, this kind of interpretation is only discovered through heightened understanding, which is a matter of individual spiritual maturing. This cannot be taught. It must be lived out.

Not long after my seminary years, I came upon the writings of Karlfried Graf Dürckheim. This was once again a "coincidence," the kind that brings to mind the saying that the definition of coincidence is "God working anonymously." Strangely enough, Dürckheim began teaching in Europe around the time of Gurdjieff's death in 1949. In a way, he picks up where the master left off. Dürckheim died in 1988, shortly after I met his primary disciples, Alphonse and Rachel Goettmann.

I have since learned that, in the last decade of his life, Dürckheim became very involved with the teachings of Orthodox Christianity. He told the Bishop of the Orthodox Church of France, Monseigneur Germain, that had he encountered it earlier in life, he would have become an Orthodox Christian. This is particularly of interest because Gurdjieff's life and work was also linked to Orthodoxy. The recent English publication of the trilogy *Gnosis: Study and Commentaries of the Esoteric Tradition of Eastern Orthodoxy*, by Boris Mouravieff, makes a strong case for the direct relationship between the Fourth Way and the Royal Way, the inner teaching of the early Church.

THE WHEEL OF METAMORPHOSIS

"The Self we discover in the experience of Hara is clearly no longer the old I but a wider, more comprehensive one. We become conscious of a new inner breadth . . . We do not lose ourselves in it but, on the contrary, truly find ourselves. A new breathing space, scope and sphere of action opens up and we realize only then how confined we had been before, how imprisoned and isolated."(13)

The inner practice that Karlfried Graf Dürckheim developed over his many years of study, travel and experience offers to contemporary seekers a way of radical transformation. Combining the insights and practices of Zen Buddhism with depth psychology and Christian mysticism, he has created a potent, practical way of inner work which thousands have undertaken.

Dürckheim centers his teaching on our rare moments of higher consciousness, those numinous experiences that he names "privileged moments" and "life's starry hours." These are unforgettable times when something greater than our usual awareness breaks through and floods us with unaccountable serenity, joy, or certainty. Such experiences call us toward a new way of living and initiate us into a different view of reality. Mystics, philosophers, saints, and esotericists of all times have pointed to these radiant moments as proof that we are more than we seem to be.

These inner events open our eyes to the higher influences present in our world. Many teachings have attempted to bring us to a near continual experience of this higher consciousness, but they all seem to suffer a similar fate. Almost as soon as these teachings have been transmitted, they become rigid and dogmatic, and the spirit gives way to the letter. Dürckheim's method begins and ends with the individual on his or her unique path. He offers no theory, no cosmology, no religious philosophy. He merely tells us in the magnificent simplicity of eastern sages that each moment is the best of opportunities for working on oneself, and he provides us with a process for the expansion of consciousness that he calls the Wheel of Metamorphosis. These are inner disciplines that each person can apply to himself or herself. Dürckheim warns us that this practice must be done continuously with concentrated awareness or it will lead nowhere. Verification and understanding come out of lived experience.

The first step on the entrance into our own mystery is the intense effort of critical watchfulness. This is a turning of the powers of our attention inwardly so that we become aware of our attitudes and their related physical expressions. This discipline is uncommonly difficult to sustain and painful to the fantasy we take ourselves to be as it requires a commitment and honesty worthy of the most severe ascetical practices. Through this daily, unrelenting exercise reminiscent of the eastern Christian teaching of the "watch of the heart" and of Gurdjieff's method of self-observation, we enter into Dürckheim's cyclical inner practice. The Wheel of Metamorphosis consists of three stages and five steps:

Stage 1—all that is contrary to our true nature must be relinquished.

step 1: the practice of critical watchfulness (Objective observation of our inner motives and attitudes that block us from experiencing higher consciousness.)

step 2: the letting go of all that stands in the way of new becoming (Releasing our tensions and behavior patterns which crystallize around the ego.)

Stage 2—that which has been relinquished must be dissolved in transcendent Being which absorbs and recreates us.

step 3: union with transcendent Being (Encountering the deeper Self, particularly through meditation.)

step 4: new becoming in accordance with the inner image that has arisen from transcendent Being (Seeking to manifest our true nature through a new relationship to ourselves and to the outside world.)

Stage 3—the newly formed core must be recognized and personal responsibility taken for its growth.

step 5: practicing this new form on a daily basis through critical watchfulness which leads us back to step one of the process (An ever deepening cycle of watchfulness—letting go—union—transformed living.)

The key to this process lies in the fact that each step contains all the others and only has meaning within the context of the continuous revolution of the wheel. We are dealing with the cyclic movement of a spiral: critical watchfulness—letting go—union—new becoming, generating ceaseless transformation.

Dürckheim names this inner practice "self-becoming." The term suggests a dynamic, natural movement which rises out of who we are, just as the flower rises out of the image contained in its seed. Clearly, intense effort remains a vital part of the journey, but Dürckheim's teaching is grounded in natural processes rooted in our life center, the place in which we are constantly created by cosmic life-forces that are identified as our Hara. For Dürckheim, higher consciousness—which he names transcendent or divine Being—seeks to manifest itself through our bodily presence. This life-force actively seeks to become conscious of itself through our awakening to our essential nature. All of the exercises, practices and insights that Dürckheim offers are meant to render us "transparent to transcendent Being." A conscious being is one through whom the divine life radiates. The personality has been made entirely permeable and obedient to essence, the subconscious has been cleansed and liberated, and the way is cleared for our higher states to express themselves through our condition of openness, receptivity, and presence in the moment.

Work on oneself is not centered on self for the sake of self. Dürckheim has a much wider panorama in view. Our efforts are meant to prepare us to reach a state where life in the service of transcendent Being becomes second nature. In discovering our own essential self, we participate in the manifestation of what can only be described as divine—the source of mercy, compassion, and conscious love.

This possibility requires work on all parts of our nature. But Dürckheim is especially insistent on the body as a key to breaking through to a greater consciousness.

CENTERING IN HARA

At the heart of his teaching, we find the ancient knowledge of Hara. The Japanese term Hara means nothing more than the physical embodiment of the original Life center in human beings. Literally, it means stomach, but that of course only refers to the general location of these forces. Hara is the very embodiment of our contact with the fundamental powers of the Greater Life manifested in us. It is a gift from life which is ours without our having earned it. But only by preserving the right center of gravity can it unfold its fullest meaning. This is achieved through correct postures, meditation, and breathing. It puts us in touch with unsuspected power that can be clearly seen in the martial arts as practiced by real masters and in exceptional moments such as when a frail person is suddenly able to lift a car from a child who has been hurt. But Dürckheim warns us that, though originally beyond good and evil, Hara becomes destructive when incorporated with a self-seeking and presumptuous ego.

Right attitude is centered in the Hara, which defines the foundation of the person. Hara represents our vital center, the earth center. To be rooted in this center is to be open to the powers of renewal of the cosmic life. This attitude, realized in a perfect way in the posture of the Buddha in meditation, is nearly the opposite to that of the Greek disc-thrower focused toward a goal and a performance (to throw the disk as far as possible). He is as unbalanced in space as the Buddha is stable and deeply rooted. The attitude of the disc-thrower perfectly symbolizes an "arrow consciousness," always aiming toward a goal, making of the body the instrument of this will to power.

Finally, in right breathing, we are breathed in by the great Life that expresses itself through our bodily presence—it breathes through us. Dürckheim teaches that breathing represents the movement of the Creative Life which, in each moment, dissolves all that threatens to harden us in order to give birth to a new form. The ego, the small, artificial self-made I, is that which must be dissolved: "For the prisoner of the I the world has no breadth. His whole consciousness at any given time is filled completely by what he sees at the moment or by whatever has taken possession of his feelings."(14)

This is not to suggest that we are to become devoid of feelings. It is quite the opposite. By remaining inwardly in contact with the vaster reality made available through Hara, our normal feelings and experiences are transmuted in such a way that they further open us to Being. Dürckheim tells us that the more a person becomes rooted in Hara, the more he or she "joyously experiences a new closeness to himself and to the world, to people and things, to nature and God—a closeness beyond the opposites of near and far, cold and heat, sympathy and antipathy as felt by the I."(15)

CRITICAL WATCHFULNESS

Dürckheim respects the human body as an expression of transcendent Being in a particular form and calls upon us to seek our right center of gravity within it. This requires work on posture, tension, and breathing. The primary practice to achieve such centering is meditation.

This fundamental exercise, however, is not to be confused with certain methods used in our New Age culture. Dürckheim tells us that "the purpose of correct practice is not to bring man to a state of tranquility but to keep him in a condition of constant watchfulness and prevent him from coming to a standstill on the Way."(16)

The energy of attention becomes a vital resource for transformation. Moreover, the fundamental effort of divided attention found in the teachings of the Fourth Way and of eastern Christianity is central to Dürckheim's inner practice: "Without the attention that collects the whole person—so that he is at the same time focused within himself and turned towards the object—no meditation is possible."(17).

This continuous awareness is maintained outside of meditation as well, and is focused on our usual behavior so as to dissolve the obstructions interfering with the possibility of radiating a vaster consciousness. Dürckheim's "critical watchfulness" refers to continual inner awareness of our behavior, in other words, to self-observation. This relentless effort is meant to lead to a growth of consciousness that provides us with a new sensitivity enabling us to perceive all deviations from our correct center.

Dürckheim identifies this center as a state wherein a person moves continuously toward his innermost nature. It is not a place but our driving force calling us home. From this center we are able to acquire a clear sense of inner direction, and above all, a "self-confidence that is independent of the world's praise or blame."(18) Without this center, we are the plaything of inner and outer forces.

Practice on ourselves, in the physical and spiritual sense, is always of two kinds. It involves both the pulling-down of everything that stands in the way of our contact with Divine Being, and the building-up of a 'form' which, by remaining accessible to its inner life, preserves this contact and affirms it in every activity in the world. (19)

Dürckheim insists that if we have become conscious of our essence, we have become conscious of our union with transcendence. But to achieve this, we need to have the courage to meet the unknown, and to "endure the mystery that cannot be conceptually comprehended—in short, to pause and inwardly dwell in that to which we are all too unaccustomed, the radiance of Divine Being."(20). Dürckheim calls upon us to risk over and over again all that we think we have understood, all that we hold onto as security.

LETTING GO

Dürckheim deals with the dominance of our artificial personality through the psycho-physical process of "letting go." His long years of study in Zen Buddhism, including eight years with Zen masters in Japan, resulted in his discovery of the unquestionable link between psychological attitudes and bodily tensions. To be released from our misperceptions is not merely a mental effort but requires dissolving the physical knots and distorted postures which express these attitudes. Clenched jaws, cramped stomachs, raised shoulders all keep us outside of the realm of essence which is the only threshold to our true becoming.

Letting go also means "forsaking the brilliance of the rational mind and entering the semi-darkness of another form of consciousness"(21). The tyranny of the intellect and of a cultural world view reduced to the surface of the five senses can be a powerful barrier to the reception of divine inspiration.

> By letting go in the right way, we learn to 'let in' and 'let happen' that which, in spite of all our ideas, projections, desires and prejudices, meets us directly in the shape of the world and comes from the constantly stirring essential being within. (22)

The practice of meditation is a permanent exercise, an intentional attitude in daily life, where each occasion reveals itself as the best one to advance on the Way. Meditation is the only place where the tool of continual vigilance is fashioned.

This kind of "watchfulness" arouses in the experience of the present moment such an acute sensitivity toward that which is false and blocks our advance on the Way that it immediately provokes a letting go, through which all meditation begins.

For instance, the awareness that one's neck and shoulders are tense due to some nervous reaction or fear can spark the effort to intentionally relax those muscles. That simple activity aligns our whole organism with its center, allowing us to breath more deeply and to relate in a different way to the event that caused the tension.

The activity of meditation itself, which empowers us to control our states and to remain open to higher influences, is taught by Dürckheim in the following manner:

POSTURE IN MEDITATION

1. Sit in the chosen position, bringing the hands together in the form of a cup gently pressed against the abdomen.

2. Lean forward and slowly straighten your spine from the bottom up. Upon reaching the head, stretch out the backbone upwardly so that it is straight and let it gently come back on itself without curving in.

3. Bring in the chin to push the nape in line with the backbone. During meditation, the back of the head points toward the ceiling as though pushing back a weight.

4. Upon exhalation, let the power of the lower stomach settle in, relaxing and dilating it so that it can take root. With this sensation of heaviness, slowly move back and forth in order to find the right position at which point the movement will stop on its own.

5. The eyes remain half-open. The gaze is neutral and rests on a point approximately one yard in front of you without fixing it.

6. Listen to your breathing, passively. Nothing moves other than the diaphragm which comes and goes. The immobility is total.

7. Upon breathing out, let go throughout your body, from head to foot. Say "I let myself go" or "let go" on each exhalation. Be sure not to let your body sag. The backbone must remain in its proper alignment and the head stay in touch with the ceiling. Contemplate your rhythm of breathing. Breathe out: let go - give yourself - surrender. Breathe in (which comes of itself): rebirth.

For beginners, the entry into this posture needs to take all the time necessary to cover these points. Perhaps ten minutes or more. But soon this posture will be so familiar that we will take it up within a few seconds.

8. We must know how to come out of the posture after meditation, without rupture from the state we have entered into. Turn the head slowly to the right and left, move the shoulders and the toes. Finally, disconnect the hands very gently, with the movement you would use to wash them. Lean forward deeply and rise upon inhalation.

All these exercises are done without effort. Never go beyond what you can do comfortably, and stop at the least ill feeling. Persons who have hypertension, cardiac troubles or weak lungs should ask the advice of their physicians before undertaking these exercises.

PROPER BREATHING

Once the diaphragm functions normally, the following
way of breathing must become habitual as it centers us
in the lower region and allows us to live always,
whatever we are doing, in a deeper attitude: when you
breathe in, the abdominal wall gently tenses and you
will feel a force naturally establishing itself there.
Breathing out, instead of letting this force go out as it
usually does, hold it in by pushing toward the lower
part of the body, on the intestines. The abdominal wall
remains in this slight tension, but be sure to keep your
breathing easy and comfortable. At the beginning,
practice this each time you think of it, then you will
find that you progressively breathe this way all day
long. Soon it will become very easy to do and this
sensation of inner fullness will not leave you.

One final word concerning breathing during
meditation: it is done freely, without interfering in any
way with its natural flow, except that the exhalation is
directed toward the lower as we have described. As we
progress, relaxation deepens to such an extent that the
breath becomes slower and almost imperceptible. A
thimble of air is all that is needed say the masters. Some
of them breathe in for a second, breathe out for the
length of another second, and between the two, lungs
empty, there is a space of ten seconds or more. It is an
extreme state of absorption and of profound
contemplation that comes of itself without our having
to force it.(23)

Dürckheim sought to awaken people to their higher selves and to the deeper dimensions of reality. Yet even as a masterful teacher, he only presented a partial picture of a state of being that cannot be expressed in words. His ultimate purpose was to serve as a signpost pointing in the direction of that which is written in our hearts and which we must each discover for ourselves.

With both Gurdjieff and Dürckheim, we learn the process of freeing ourselves from the mental, emotional and even physical prison in which we live. Both concentrate on that attention which reveals us to ourselves; on that release from the stream of thoughts and anxieties that run our lives; and on a relationship to the body that makes it a partner in our spiritual development (Dürckheim with his background in Zen Buddhism and Gurdjieff as a teacher of sacred Sufi dance). Gurdjieff's teaching is primarily a psychological effort tailored to the western scientific mindset. Dürckheim's approach is more eastern and reaches into the intuitive side of our being. In a sense, they represent work on two aspects of our nature. Ultimately, one teaching cannot go without the other anymore than we can do without a right or left brain. There are many techniques from various traditions that are helpful to the spiritual journey, regardless of one's belief system. The application of these methods is to some degree related to a person's characteristics and temperament as well as to their physical condition. Yet there are a few fundamentals that have proven over time to be critical to the effort of spiritual awakening. We have seen, for instance, how the use of attention is a beginning step in stabilizing our inner world so that we may eventually find its deep spiritual center. We have also seen how meditation has a profound impact on body, mind, and spirit.

The Christian tradition, as with all other major religious traditions, has its own powerful methods for spiritual development and many of them are eminently applicable to our life today. Some of them need to be decoded from outdated language and life-styles, others need to be refined with some of the holistic insights of transpersonal psychology. In any event, our age requires experientially based methods that work for all the different kinds of individuals in our pluralistic culture. We cannot begin with the assumptions that the old traditions hold. For many people, the very concept of God is foreign, confusing, and incomprehensible. We live in a time of great crisis and we need strong medicines that will work in the chaos of our daily lives.

The teachings of Gurdjieff and Dürckheim leave unspoken the living out of one's life at the next stage of development once we have made contact with higher consciousness. This contact engenders its own unique inspiration within the forms of our particular life. Each person is responsible for the understanding that he or she acquires in this way. I am not suggesting that all methods are relative, that we can pick and choose as in a grocery store. There are absolutes at the core of Truth. But if all the spokes in the wheel lead to a common hub, then we find that Truth is One regardless of method and tradition.

VIII

Christianity as Inner Practice

After having rejected Christianity as an impotent, superficial shadow of its former self, I eventually came to embrace it. In my experience, the Christian path is the universal spiritual way that enlightened individuals of all traditions travel. The parallels between esoteric and eastern teachings in relation to Christian practice point toward an all-embracing element—union with the divine—in a religion that has too often been a means of separating some members of the human race from others.

The lives of the Christian mystics are clear testimonials to the power and nature of the teachings of the Christ. These individuals were living witnesses to the truth inherent in the sayings that have come down to us. The mystics did not merely write about this truth, or speak of it to others, but *became* the truth. The contemporary gatekeepers of Christianity can hardly remember the fourteenth century mystic Jacob Boheme or others like him, and yet their lives are vivid proof that radical inner change is the heartbeat of Christian revelation.

THE TEACHER

Jesus of Nazareth is seen as the incarnation of God, of the spiritual essence of Creation. He is called the *Logos* or the Word because he is the expression of the intent of creation. If this idea seems extravagant to you, consider that the whole purpose of this religion, and of virtually all others as well, is to lead each one of us into becoming a similar manifestation. We are all meant to become "children of God," aware that we are one with the mysterious forces that generated existence itself.

The presence of the God-man among us is not so supernatural and discontinuous with our reality when we stop to consider that ordinary life is supernatural as well. We take for granted the fact that birds build nests for their young; that our cellular structure is constantly renewing itself (we are literally not the people we were a year ago); that we are at this moment spinning sixty-five thousand miles an hour around the sun. We make it mundane, boring and empty. We strip it of its intrinsic sacredness by reducing our self-worth to achievement or the gathering of material possessions. Our life becomes a matter of doing and getting rather than of being and becoming. Then religious teachings, spiritual masters, and the idea of a universal God are dislocated from their integral place at the heart of reality.

Jesus was called by his followers "the first born" and he invited everyone to enter upon his way in order to find their own consciousness of being a part of God. To accomplish this all-important task, he wiped the slate clean: no priests, no ritual worship, no code of laws, no group morality. Jesus abolished religion and tore down the walls separating us from a direct, spiritual encounter with the divine—within all of life and within ourselves.

He is called the "Way" because his life described a path with his own blood, tears, and joy. This path includes care for all, uncompromising dedication to the values of Eternal Truth, self-annihilation for rebirth into a higher state. He is called *Christos* (the anointed one) because his human consciousness gave way to his divine consciousness. The universal Spirit, the breath of God, lived within his temporal body of flesh.

THE TEACHING

Christianity is not the worship of a cult figure. It is the very process of transformation that makes a human being another Christos, an awakened child of the Creator. Perhaps few of us will achieve his level of oneness with the cosmic forces that brought all things into being, but that may be because few of us are willing to sacrifice and love as fully as he did. We can each be temples of the Spirit, new creations liberated from our pettiness and blindness who are empowered to bless the world around us. But how badly do we want these things over the distractions, conveniences and enticements offered to us at every instant? Christian teaching describes both crucifixion and resurrection. These words are not only metaphors, nor are they simply events dating back to antiquity. Rather they are concepts that apply to the human ego, the one thing that stands in the way of our development.

The ego is grounded in unevolved natural forces (the survival instinct, infantile self-centeredness), in unconscious behavior (parental imitation, environmental influence) and in imagination (fantasy of self-importance). It is an impostor that is the source of our misery and distorted relationships to others.

The Christ says: Cut it loose, jump off the cliff of your false identity, don't turn back, or more biblically, "sell all you have and follow me." This is a radical, unadulterated, all-consuming teaching. At the same time, this strong spirituality is centered on active compassion, irrepressible hope, and ecstatic joy. It encompasses the yin and yang, the death and rebirth recognized by all visionaries at the core of reality itself.

Severe ascetics and fanatic followers of the Christian tradition have often violated the tone and purity of this old teaching. But it is easy to find the authentic reflection of a life in Christ among Christianity's best representatives, such as Francis of Assisi, Teresa of Avila, and, in our day, Thomas Merton. The great saints and mystics were lovers of God and therefore lovers of all beings. One of them, the twelfth-century monk Bernard of Clairvaux, expressed Christian inner work with sublime simplicity: "The measure of love is to love beyond measure."

WATCHFULNESS

One of the keys to opening the door leading to our true

nature is found in the most common element in our psyche: attention. As we saw in previous chapters, early Christian teachers recognized it as central to spiritual development.

An elementary definition of attention might be that it is a focusing of our energy onto a subject of interest. We all know instinctively when this inner power waxes and wanes. We can remember from school days how often we found our attention wandering off into realms of fantasy or to the scenery outside the window. With maturity, we may have found it necessary to develop that muscle of concentration to keep ourselves engaged on a particular task. What many people have not realized is that this same intangible power of attention is critical to our spiritual awakening. If we let it dissipate into the countless distractions of life, we will find that our life-force is drained, unavailable for our ultimate task of conscious existence.

Most of us lack the self-awareness that is required to realize the dignity of being human. From the character driving down the highway more focused on his daydreams than on the road and the lives of those around him to the thoughtless parent who shames his child, this lack of inner attention is the cause of our continual stumbling.

Self-awareness and the subsequent encounter with the divine are rare in human behavior because they require energy. We squander most of the "psychic gold" of our attention on everything from fidgeting to outbursts of anger. Remember how worn out you felt from just one explosion of rage? It can wipe out a whole day's ration of energy, as can constant talking, daydreaming, worrying, and other energy leaks.

A person who wants to awaken to spiritual reality needs to value this energy that must be restored on a daily basis. If a twenty-four hour period is a microcosm of a lifetime, we can clearly see that the habit of wasting our life-force can turn an entire existence into a lost opportunity.

Watchfulness requires that we pay attention to the thoughts, impulses and desires vying for expression and satisfaction. This attention itself may prevent them from taking control. Through this effort we establish a stable foundation for our inner transformation.

Nothing can be accomplished if we are not dependable or mindful of our commitment. We cannot be of use to ourselves or to anyone else if we are constantly tossed about by the waves of our inner chaos. We gain a "clear sight" when we lift ourselves above the thoughts and feelings that struggle with each other within us. This is not merely a psychological trick, but clears the ground and makes room to receive the inflow of a higher power.

Christ, understood not as a man from the Judean hill country but as the incarnation of the conscious core of all creation, tells us in uncompromising terms how essential it is that we find our center, that we abide in him: "He who abides in me, and I in him, he it is that bears much fruit."

To abide in Christ is not a matter of opinion about religious beliefs, but of alignment with the very nature of reality, with our deepest forces.

The Belgian priest and theologian, Louis Evely, summed up the mission of the founder of Christianity in this way: "Jesus' greatest liberation is to have liberated us from religion! He wanted us all to have free, direct and joyful access to God."

THE FEMININE SIDE OF CHRISTIANITY

Christianity has been weighed down for centuries by a harsh patriarchal worldview that has rendered its teachings virtually impotent. But the hierarchies and male-oriented images of the Creator are distortions that were added to the religion according to customs of the cultures in which it flourished. The fact is that Christianity has a critical feminine element that cannot be overlooked.

The figure of Mary has long been present to the consciousness of Christians as a balancing out of the concepts of the divine and of our encounter with it. Though popular belief turned her into an intercessor, she is much more than this. Mary is an archetype of the human soul and its relationship to the cosmos. Consider the following excerpt taken from *The Beyond Within* originally published in French by Alphonse and Rachel Goettmann:

Mary is the archetype of all contemplative meditation. That which characterizes her the most is the sentence from Scripture: "Mary kept all these things, pondering them in her heart." Mary is Virgin because she is "dispossessed of all the worries of the world" as is sung in the ancient liturgy. Her flesh is silent in immobility— emptied of all chatter of the mind, of passions and earthly attractions, her will is annihilated: "Behold, I am the handmaid of the Lord; let it be to me according to your word." It is at the heart of this supreme letting go in surrender that Mary opens herself to the uncreated Silence. It is into this virginity that we enter through meditation; the famous Void of Zen has no other meaning, even if the words are missing to express this. To become virgin, we must enter into silence, the emptiness of absolute letting go of all dependence, the sacrifice of our will and of every desire.

Then, in the depths of this human silence, will descend the Silence of God. Through her total self-surrender, Mary has opened herself to the total self-surrender of God. Her virginity calls forth maternity and every true meditation becomes an Annunciation. Each time my heart opens to this Silent Abyss of the Uncreated, the voice of the Angel says: "Hail, O favored one, the Lord is with you!" To be Virgin and Mother inseparably is the summit of human accomplishment and maturity; this is meditation's pearl of great price which ties in one sheaf all the divine mysteries. Mary is its purest expression, the first one of Humanity to realize that to which we are all called. (1)

This material, written by Orthodox Christians, clearly points to a much more profound understanding of Mary and of the feminine element at the heart of Christianity. The allegorical and symbolic interpretation of these ancient teachings offers the contemporary seeker a whole new way of applying their wisdom to his or her life.

The male-dominated images of Christianity burned into our subconscious through the images of Michelangelo and so many other artists hired to express the Church's dogma need to be cleaned out of our psyche. The rediscovery of the feminine dimension of spirituality is essential for salvaging the original intent of these teachings and for surfacing their dynamic value for all who seek a deeper encounter with Reality.

The absurdity of reducing cosmic mysteries to gender types is all too obvious in our day. It is high time to claim the truth of these teachings from the more primitive and man-made (literally) mindset of the past. Consider, for instance, the business of celibacy that is currently thinning out the ranks of Catholic priests. This requirement was not a commandment from the Christ, but was instituted through a pope's decree some eleven hundred years later. Priests of the Eastern Christian tradition, whose roots are the oldest in Christianity, are allowed to wed and bring up families. These kinds of arbitrary decisions, sanctified through the pomp and circumstance of powerful and often dehumanizing hierarchies, are responsible for the anti-feminine stance that has soured this particular religion.

The fact is that the only followers who did not abandon the crucified man on Golgotha were women! And the first to discover the empty tomb that generated the faith known as Christianity were also women. Just as we find the concepts of the Creator evolving from a tribal god appeased with bloody sacrifices to a universal power characterized by unconditional love, so the feminine aspect of God continues to evolve.

For centuries, Mary was the only image of the nurturing dimension of the creative force of the universe. Without her, the icons of God and of Jesus began to petrify into distant, judgmental figures. Mary's gentleness gave the people hope in the face of the all-consuming, terrifying power of the Uncreated.

In our holistic age, we are able to go a step further. Breaking through the male images of the past, we discover that the word "God" comes from a Sanskrit term meaning "that which is invoked." There is no beard here, no angry and jealous Superman. There is only the dynamic, caring Presence that heals the lonely, lost and frightened human soul.

ILLUMINED PRESENCE

Spiritual teachers of nearly every tradition tell us that learning how not to respond to external stimulus is a necessary step for inner development. The effect of not reacting to an external event does not imply a cold, disconnected relationship to life. Detachment, as understood in the classical mystical tradition, is not removal from life but from one's own uncontrolled emotions and attitudes.

In this age where we are relentlessly bombarded by

images designed to manipulate us, the ancient method of the "watch of the heart" is most valuable in saving us from drowning in a sea of over-stimulation.

The teachings gathered in the *Philokalia* from the great spiritual masters of early Christianity, offer specific ways of developing the power of freeing ourselves from the hypnotism of external stimuli. Turned inwardly, attention stands guard over images coming in from without and thoughts arising from within. Persistent awareness insures that both stimuli are kept from further influencing our behavior. For once the image is allowed to penetrate within, it is on the way to being materialized into action. I am referring here to actions that are contrary to our aims of spiritual development, such as lust, violence, greed.

Early spiritual masters list the following capacities developed through inner watchfulness:

—The guarding of the intellect
—Continuous insight into the heart's depths
—Stillness of mind unbroken even by thoughts which appear to be good
—The capacity to be empty of all thought

External reality now comes to us without our filters of expectations, prejudices, and judgments that otherwise mar our view. The experts on inner warfare tell us that we should wage this war with a focused and united will that disperses fantasies. The intellect then no longer pursues them "like a child deceived by some conjurer" (*Philokalia*, saying 105).

The masters further claim that such watchfulness gives us knowledge, enlightenment, and instruction previously unattainable by our intellect while we were still "walking in the murk of passions and dark deeds, in forgetfulness and in the confusion of chaos" (saying 116).

The critical issue is to recognize that this internal work makes it possible for us to act from a place of enlightened insight rather than from automatic reaction. Though this inner work does contain an element of becoming *hermetically sealed*, it must not be confused with disinterest in the needs and troubles of the world. Never before has humanity found itself in an environment of constant manipulation, from subliminal political messages to the stirring of the desire for food when the stomach is not hungry. The spiritual warfare of old—against the "powers and principalities of the air"—is now a literal reality as the airwaves are flooded by many images whose influence is often demonic.

Most of us cannot escape to a community free from the endless downpour from the mass media. Few of us can influence this leviathan in a direction that is positive for humanity. So we are left with the obligation of following the inner journey in the midst of these random and sometimes dangerous forces. Maintaining a focus on the process within allows us to navigate through treacherous waters. For the masters I have invoked here, this effort of watchfulness is fueled by a life of prayer. In fact, they all suggest that a time comes when the act of inner vigilance fuses with the act of prayer. This fusion is a state of illumined presence that perceives the transcendental in the transient. Here is the pearl of great price sought after by spiritual seekers.

PURITY OF HEART

Let us now examine more closely the meaning of two crucial words that have surfaced throughout this book: attention and watchfulness. They are the keys to unlocking the heart and discovering what is written within it from the beginning of time.

Teachers of early Christianity define attention as a stillness of heart unbroken by any thought. This is accomplished through watchfulness which is a continual observance of thought at the "entrance" of the heart. Watchfulness is the effort of constant awareness of the thoughts, images and desires stimulated from within and from without. This awareness keeps them from automatically claiming our full attention and taking control of our will.

The clarity of attention sustained by the watch of the heart leads to an inner stability that produces an even greater intensification of watchfulness. This distancing of inner and outer stimuli from the core of our being engenders a unique quietude and serenity without which there is no spiritual consciousness.

According to the masters of the inner spiritual warfare, we can further define the stages of this necessary watchfulness:

1. watchfulness closely scrutinizes every mental image or provocation
2. frees the heart from the endless distraction of thoughts
3. continually invokes the help of higher spiritual

powers

4. keeps us mindful of our mortality

5. fixes our gaze upon spiritual reality and places the material world in proper perspective.

The end result is the inner state that Christ called purity of heart and which allows one to "see God." Surely this witnessing of the sacred, this encounter with that which created us, is the purpose of all religions.

Clearly, we can deduce that this purity of heart is not a moral condition (although that is a natural result of our transformation), but rather a state of presence that incorporates awareness of our moment by moment condition—from thoughts to muscle tensions—and relentlessly focuses on the spiritual reality beyond the visible. This "remembrance of God" is not merely an awareness of that vaster presence akin to the cosmic radiation behind all matter, the remnant of the *Big Bang* phenomenon as scientists now suggest. This inner consciousness, free from all other stimuli, is unbroken contemplation, that is, continual prayer. There are no words, no thoughts, only a "naked intent," a burning love for that which first loved us.

In the previous chapters, we have studied the degrees of prayer, the self-observation of Gurdjieff and the meditative attitude of Dürckheim, along with certain classic methods of Christian spirituality. Now we reach the summit where the mystics of all traditions unite in a common knowledge, a oneness of consciousness and being. Here all the teachings and practices melt away and the individual is consumed with the reality uncovered at the core of his or her being.

This state of knowing is both serene and blazing with unconditional love. This is where Christianity makes its special contribution to human evolution. We are no longer dealing with abstract thought or even enlightened understanding (the god of the philosophers). The furnace of transformation is *agape*, or conscious, unconditional love. The infinite silence and omnipresence of the *Tao*, as eastern wisdom has called it, has been penetrated; the riddle of *Advaita* (non-duality in the midst of seeming duality) has been solved; and, in Christian terms, the spirit of the resurrected Christ has revealed itself as the very root of our being.

Having cleaned the window of our inner self from all the impurities we know so well, an eternal sun now shines through us. The intense effort of keeping that window clean (the watch of the heart) is now transmuted into ecstatic surrender to the unnamable light that fills our mind, heart and soul.

Few of us can sustain that state of blissful consciousness, but every one of us is called to seek for it as it is the very purpose of our existence. The universe came into being in order to know itself. We are the witnesses of its awesome wonder and the caretakers of its countless forms. In every moment, we make the choice to raise ourselves to that level of awareness or to descend into the darkness of confusion and unhappiness. All around us, we see the results of the latter condition.

Throughout this book, the process of transformation has been expressed in a variety of ways. In the end, it is up to you in your particular situation, at a particular moment, to enter the liberated state that leads to your transfiguration. Become watchful, quiet your mind and body, turn the attention of your heart in humility and yearning toward the Mystery that is your source.

The poet Rumi tells us to "return to the root of the root of your Self." All revelation and objective knowledge guide us to inward wisdom. But beyond that point, in order to achieve radical transformation into beings illumined by unconditional love, we must each make the efforts tailored to the requirements of the moment. What is in the way right now? Is it negative feelings or thoughts? Is it a case of mistaken identity, where we take ourselves to be what we have invented or what is claiming our desires? Is it fascination with inward or outward images that obscure the radiance of divine light? Is it the arrogance of the rational mind against the intuitive insight, or merely infantile selfishness wanting its needs met?

We become clean with the healing (relaxing) of our nervous system which in turn makes it possible to see reality from a higher vantage point. We become changed when our sense of self expands and opens in humble receptivity to that which called us into being. We become fulfilled when we are empowered to act as vehicles of the eternal love that created life and that requires you and I to manifest its will upon planet Earth.

IMPLICATIONS

What are some implications of such a transformed life? I will list a few in random order without regard as to whether they are mundane or spectacular. For it is from the plain fabric of ordinary life that spiritual transmutation occurs.

1. *Stop hurrying*: those of us who are victims of this dreadful dis-ease know that it is a habit that is dangerous to the health of the body. But it is even more so for the health of the spirit as it throws us entirely off course. Frenzied activity or hyperactive thinking create a noise in our mind and sinews that utterly obliterates the consciousness of the Presence of God. "Be still and know that I Am God" remains one of the great revelations of the Old Testament.

2. *Let go*: we continually find ourselves faced with situations that we resist or resent. The capacity to release that tension, physically and emotionally, opens us to new possibilities. Our momentary desires are transcended and we become available for new insight.

3. *Accept*: this is a supreme act of surrendering our will to a higher one that brought us into the world. This effort teaches humility, endurance, and a liberation from fantasies. Karlfried Graf Dürckheim tells us that to accept the unacceptable is the most powerful factor in spiritual transformation.

4. *Make time*: early morning or late evening have always been considered prime quality time for penetrating the depths of the spirit. While the world sleeps, a person in meditation or quiet reflection can experience extraordinary moments of regeneration.

5. *Value the moment*: encounters with other people, waiting at a traffic light, the office coffee break are often passed over and taken for granted. But a moment of remembrance can illuminate the most ordinary event. This is especially true in relationship to other people where spirit can meet spirit.

6. *Separate*: we are not our thoughts or emotions, however strong their pull may be. Nor are we our ambitions and dreams. We are the background awareness in which they occur. That consciousness can ultimately unite us with the divine.

7. *Recognize the invisible in the visible*: the sacred is everywhere and everything. This is no religious doctrine, but scientific fact. Everything that is comes from the explosion of supernovas and from the original Big Bang that happened everywhere, all at once. There is mystery upon mystery in the smallest pebble, let alone in human beings who can ponder the cause of their arising.

8. *Do not fear*: our work requires that we step into the unknown and trust that we are received with open arms. To shrink back from a return to our source is to die prior to burial. Fear turns away from the yearning in our heart that will reunite us with our true identity, in which there is no darkness.

TRUSTING THE UNIVERSE

Nowadays, we hear a great deal about co-dependency, the

wounded inner child, and dysfunctional families. Psychologists such as John Bradshaw have brought to the surface a rather stunning fact about modern life: our society is filled with emotionally crippled individuals who were traumatized in their early years.

Whether these persons were victims of sexual abuse, violent alcoholics, or the tragedy of divorce, they all carry deep scars that incapacitate the primary building block of a healthy personality—the ability to trust. Across all socio-economic lines, regardless of academic degrees, these deeply hurt individuals have lost contact with a fundamental faith in existence itself.

Support groups, entire libraries of material, and workshops of all kinds are addressing these problems. Television talk shows seem to specialize in airing the intimate agony of adults whose inner child is still bleeding. Certainly, many of these efforts will go a long way to heal those silent and not-so-silent screams that dominate people's psychology. But that is not enough.

The experts tell us that the cornerstone of healthy development is a natural trust. We come into this world so utterly helpless that the nurturing love and protection of a parent is an absolute necessity, not a nice luxury if it can be fit into the schedule. This relationship is an exact parallel to our relationship with that mysterious, unnamable power called "God." The extent to which we can surrender ourselves into the "arms" of destiny in the certainty that unconditional love will support us even through death is the measure of how fully we will live the few decades allotted to us on this planet.

The trouble is that we are not merely victims of difficult childhoods that have robbed some of us of our innate ability to trust. We are victims of a society aggressively bent on imposing its view of reality upon us. And this worldview has no room for vulnerability, trust, or even the hope that love sustains the universe.

As consumers, we are easy bait for the sharks roaming the sea of our culture. We have all seen what happens to the prey caught in the midst of a feeding frenzy. There is little left when the beasts have satisfied their obsessive hunger. This is true for our bank accounts and for our souls as well.

The subliminal, and often overt messages of the media define our sense of manhood, womanhood, success and failure. The sharks of our culture who are masters at getting their fingers into our psyches have replaced the Madonna who symbolized total spiritual trust ("let it be done to me according to your will") for that other Madonna who symbolizes the "get it while you can" mentality of a hopelessly materialistic society.

What then is there left to trust? Is it possible to escape the mistaken sense of safety found in a cynical relationship to life? Many people believe that this is the only intelligent way to see things. But to live in such a way is not a matter of being practical. It is a state akin to asphyxiation. Our birthright is to live in peace, joy and trust. Others before us have proven that the harshness of life need not keep us from these gifts of existence. That is why poets and artists (lovers of beauty, that is), are so important. They are cries in a wilderness of advertisements, sound bites, and despair.

The teachers of wisdom from all the world's spiritual traditions urge us to take the risk of trusting the ultimate goodness of the universe. Trust in the face of all the contradictions. Trust in spite of trouble and pain. Trust even though you have been betrayed again and again. Trust because after the winter snows comes the sweetness of spring. Trust because within the noise and tumult of human life there is a Silence that heals and renews and inspires.

Conclusion

We have seen that the central ideas in religious teachings are the same: awakening to our spiritual nature and its roots in the unfathomable depths of the sacred. Our becoming aware of this reality at the core of our being generates the process of our transformation.

Why is transformation desirable? The answer is simple: each of us senses our potential for goodness, whether it manifests in the form of generosity, forgiveness, or self-sacrifice. We will remain unsatisfied and unfulfilled to the degree that we are incapable of letting these qualities blossom within us. Our only true failure is in not incarnating this capacity.

When we begin to overcome self-centeredness and its endless requirements, we find ourselves available to be of service to the life around us. A ripple effect is caused by our evolution, one whose impact we can never calculate. Just as a brutal parent damages his child who will then be likely to abuse his own children, so too does the influence of kindness radiate down through the generations. But this is much more than an attempt to be nice once in a while. The power of self-transcendence comes from our receptivity to the spiritual forces present at the heart of creation.

Self-transcendence liberates us from the baggage of the past, lifts us out of the ambitions and fears of the ego, gives us joy and hope even when outer circumstances seem hopeless, and opens wide our heart to other beings.

This transformation is our birthright and our duty. Imagine the new face of humanity if each person took responsibility for this lifelong effort. Consider the changes in political decisions, in economic priorities, in the treatment of children and of the elderly. The destiny of the entire world population could be affected along with the welfare of our planet if enough individuals made the necessary efforts to nurture their spiritual consciousness. We know only too well what the other option is, with its effects of near apocalyptic devastation through greed and violence.

We each have a choice to make, whether to follow the easy road of indulging the whims of our infantile self-centeredness or whether to resist the automatic current and begin our journey toward a higher place where unconditional love reigns. We are not helpless to save ourselves from self-destruction, nor to save the earth and its inhabitants from the plagues that threaten to consume us all. The effort begins with ourselves. Then miracles can happen.

A COMMON THREAD

From the religious experiences of the first civilizations to the latest insights in psychotherapy, we can detect a common thread that connects us with the human yearnings of every century and culture. That unifying link is the effort to encounter the sacred. Regardless of the symbols and stories through which it is presented, this intimate and transforming experience is available to every human being. All rituals, laws, and dogmas are secondary to this regenerating event that takes place in the depths of our being.

We are created to become more than we now are. Out of the earth of our natural selfishness and survival instincts can arise the flower of a new consciousness: the awareness of our oneness with all of life and of our destiny as caretakers of creation. We are the only beings on this planet that are capable of being conscious witnesses to and intentional servants of life in all its wondrous forms.

Religion is not philosophy or metaphysics. Nor is it doctrine and hierarchy. Religion is encounter, growth, merger. We are one family, united by an indefinable Love that guides and sustains us. We are one with the creatures of earth, one with the spiritual masters of all times and places, one with the Creator that our amazing technology will never uncover, dissect, or pigeonhole. This is our true dignity as human beings and we are meant to discover it and live it out within the framework of our every day existence. Here begins and here ends the purpose of religion. All else is symbol, artifice or deviation. One thing is necessary—awakening to our true selves where the secrets of life and death have been written. That is our personal salvation and the salvation of our world.

Notes

Chapter 1

1 Alphonse Goettmann, *Dialogue on the Path of Initiation: An Introduction to the Life and Thought of Karlfried Graf Dürckheim*, trans. Theodore and Rebecca Nottingham, (New York: Globe Press Books, 1992). p.53.

2 C.G. Jung and C. Kerenyi, *Essays on Science and Mythology*, trans. R.F.C. Hull, rev. ed. (New York: Harper Torchbooks, 1963), p. 1.

3 Thorkild Jacobsen, *The Treasures of Darkness* (New Haven: Yale University Press, 1976), p. 5.

4 G.S. Kirk, *Myth: Its Meaning and Functions in Ancient and other Cultures* (Berkeley: University of California Press, 1970), p. 264.

5 *Ibid.*, p. 265.

6 Kerenyi, *Essays on Science and Mythology*.

7 Kirk, *Myth: Its Meaning and Functions*, p. 89.

8 Jacobsen, *The Treasures of Darkness*, p. 5.

9 Ernst Cassirer, *The Philosophy of Symbolic Form*, trans. Ralph Manheim, vol. 2 (New Haven: Yale University Press, 1963), p. 41.

10 Johs. Pedersen, Israel: *Its Life and Culture* (London:

Oxford University Press, 1946), p. 146.

11 H. Wheeler Robinson, *Corporate Personality in Ancient Israel* (Philadelphia: Fortress Press, 1964), p. 40.

12 John Skinner, *Prophecy and Religion* (Cambridge: University Press, 1951), p. 215.

13 Albert C. Knudson, *The Prophetic Movement in Israel* (New York: Abingdon Press, 1966), p. 137.

14 Skinner, *Prophecy and Religion*, p. 198.

15 Joseph Campbell, T*he Hero of a Thousand Faces* (Princeton: Princeton University Press, 1968), p. 270.

16 *Ibid.*, p. 388.

17 *Ibid.*, p. 389.

18 *Ibid.*

Chapter 2

1 Thomas Merton, *Love and Living*, (New York: Bantam Books, 1979), p. 176.

2 *Ibid.*, p. 179.

Chapter 3

1 Evelyn Underhill, *The Essentials of Mysticism* (New York: E. P. Dutton, 1920), p. 12.

2 *Ibid.*, p. 15.

3 Evelyn Underhill, *Practical Mysticism* (New York: E. P. Dutton, 1943), p. xi.

4 *Ibid.*, p. 3.

5 *Ibid.*, p.

6 G. I. Gurdjieff, *Views From the Real World* (New York: E. P. Dutton, 1975), p. 153.

7 Jacob Needleman, *Lost Christianity* (New York: Bantam Books, 1982), p. 131.

8 Maurice Nicoll, *The New Man* (New York: Penguin Books, 1979), p. 143.

9 Thomas Merton, *New Seeds of Contemplation* (Toronto: New Directions, 1961), p. 126.

10 *Ibid.*, p. 127.

11 *Ibid.*, p. 130.

12 P. D. Ouspensky, *In Search of the Miraculous* (New York: Harcourt Brace Jovanovich, 1977), p. 53.

13 Merton, *New Seeds of Contemplation*, p. 208.

14 Claudio Naranjo and Robert E. Ornstein, *On the Psychology of Meditation* (New York: Viking Press, 1971), p. 176.

15 Merton, *New Seeds of Contemplation*, p. 7.

16 *Ibid.*, p. 8

17 *Ibid.*

18 *Ibid.*, p. 228.

19 Needleman, *Lost Christianty*, p. 194.

20 John White, ed., *The Highest State of Consciousness* (Garden City: Anchor Books, 1972), p. xv.

CHAPTER 4

1 Thomas Merton, *New Seeds of Contemplation* (New

York: New Directions, 1962), p. 25.

2   John J. Higgins, *Thomas Merton On Prayer* (New York: Image Books, 1975), p. 19.

3   *Ibid.*, p. 53.

4   Douglas V. Steere, *Prayer and Worship* (New York: Hazen Books on Religion, 1938), p. 10.

5   *Ibid.*, p. 15.

6   M. Basil Pennington, *Daily We Touch Him: Practical Religious Experiences* (New York: Images Books, 1977), p. 110.

7   *Ibid.*, p. 80.

8   Perry LeFrevre, ed. *Understandings of Prayer* (Philadelphia: The Westminster Press, 1981), p. 34.

9   *Ibid.*, p. 185.

10   E. Kadloubovsky and G. E. H. Palmer, trans., *Writings from the Philokalia on Prayer of the Heart* (London: Faber and Faber, 1979), p. 32.

11   Thomas R. Kelly, *A Testament of Devotion* (New York: Harper & Row, 1941), p. 32.

12   *Ibid.*, p. 41.

13   Higgins, *Thomas Merton on Prayer,* p. 83.

14   Evelyn Underhill, *Concerning the Inner Life* (New York: E. P. Dutton & Co, Inc., 1926), p. 99.

15   *Ibid.*

16   *Ibid.*, p. 102.

17   M. Basil Pennington, "The Many Lives and Stirring

Times of Thomas Merton" *National Catholic Reporter* 21 (January 1985):20.

18 Grace Adolphsen Brame, *Receptive Prayer* (St. Louis: CBP Press, 1981), p. 31.

19 *Ibid.*, p. 33.

20 *Ibid.*, p. 37.

21 *Ibid.*, p. 51.

22 *Ibid.*, p. 82.

23 M. Basil Pennington, *Daily We Touch Him* (Garden City: Doubleday, 1977), p. 46.

24 Jean-Nicholas Grou, *How to Pray,* trans. Joseph Dalby (Greenwood, South Carolina: The Attic Press, 1982).

25 Thomas Kelly, *Reality of the Spiritual World* (Wallingford: Pendle Hill), p. 36.

26 Anonymous, *A Guide to True Peace* (New York: Pendle Hill, 1960), p. 33.

27 Douglas V. Steere, *On Beginning from Within* (New York: Harper & Brothers, 1943), p. 79.

28 *Ibid.*, p. 108

29 *Ibid.*, p. 135.

30 *Ibid.*, p. 86.

31 Kelly, *A Testament of Devotion,* p. 39.

32 Underhill, *Concerning the Inner Life,* p. 58.

33 Alphonse Goettmann, "Know Yourself: Toward a Transparent Consciousness," trans. Theodore J. Nottingham, *Le Chemin* 14 (Winter 1991),p. 76.

34 Jean-Pierre De Caussade, *The Sacrament of the Present Moment* (Paris: Desclee De Brouwer, 1966), p. 22.

35 *Ibid.*, p. 41.

Chapter 5

1 Maurice Goguel, *The Birth of Christianity*, trans. H. C. Snape (New York: The Macmillan Company, 1954), p. 347.

2 Johannes Weiss, *Earliest Christianity*, trans. Frederick C. Grant, vol. 2 (New York: Harper Torchbooks, 1959), p. 793.

3 Maurice Nicoll, *The Mark* (London: Watkins, 1981), p. 94.

4 Alphonse Goettmann, "Itineraire pour une renaissance: la parabole du semeure" *Le Chemin* 15 (Summer 1992),p. 52.

5 Alphonse and Rachel Goettmann, *Where Silence Dwells: Christian Witness and Practice*, trans. Theodore J. Nottingham, unpublished manuscript.

Chapter 7

1 Merrily E. Taylor, ed., *Remembering Pyotr Demianovitch Ouspensky* (New Haven: Yale University Library, 1978), p. 8.

2 P. D. Ouspensky, *The Psychology of Man's Possible Evolution* (New York: Vintage Books, 1974), p. 11.

3 *Ibid.*, p. 12.

4 P. D. Ouspensky, *In Search of the Miraculous* (New York: Harcourt Brace Jovanovich, 1977), p. 53.

5 *Ibid.*, p. 54.

6 Ouspensky, *The Psychology of Man's Possible Evolution*, p.29.

7 Kathleen Riordan Speeth, *The Gurdjieff Work* (Berkeley: And/Or Press, 1976), p. 43.

8 Ouspensky, *The Psychology of Man's Possible Evolution*, p. 44.

9 Rodney Collin, *The Theory of Celestial Influence* (London: Watkins Books Ltd, 1980), p. 208.

10 Maurice Nicoll, *Psychological Commentaries on the Teachings of Gurdjieff-Ouspensky* (London: Watkins, 1957), p.416.

11 *Ibid.*, p. 1688.

12 Rodney Collin, *The Mirror of Light* (London: Watkins, 1959), p. 82.

13 Karlfried Graf Dürckheim, *Hara: The Vital Center of Man* (London: Mandala Books, 1984), p. 110.

14 *Ibid.*

15 *Ibid.*, p. 111.

16 Karlfried Graf Dürckheim, *The Way of Transformation: Daily Life as Spiritual Exercise* (London: Allen & Unwin, 1988) p. 27.

17 *Ibid.*, p. 37.

18 *Ibid.*, p. 51.

19 *Ibid.*, p. 44.

20 *Ibid.*, p. 65.

21 *Ibid.*, p. 25.

22 *Ibid.*, p. 81.

23 Alphonse and Rachel Goettmann, T*he Beyond Within:
    Initiation into Christian Meditation,* trans. Theodore and
    Rebecca Nottingham, (St Meinrad: Abbey Press,
    1992), p.76.

Chapter 8

1 Goettmann, *The Beyond Within: Initiation into Christian
   Meditation,* p. 105.

Bibliography

Brame, Grace Adolphsen. *Receptive Prayer*. St. Louis: CBP Press, 1981.

Brother Lawrence. *The Practice of the Presence of God*. Nashville: Thomas Nelson Publishers, 1981.

Campbell, Joseph. *The Hero of A Thousand Faces*. Princeton: Princeton University Press, 1968.

Capps, Walter H., ed. *Ways of Understanding Religion*. New York: MacMillan Company, 1972.

Cassirer, Ernst. *The Philosophy of Symbolic Forms*. Translated by Ralph Manheim. Vols. 2 and 3. New Haven: Yale University Press, 1963.

Castle, E. B. *Approach to Quakerism*. London: Bannisdales Press, 1961.

Collin, Rodney. *The Mirror of Light*. London: Watkins Books, 1959.

_____. *The Theory of Celestial Influence*. London: Watkins, 1980.

Day, Albert. *Discipline and Discovery*. Nashville: The Parthenon Press, 1961.

De Caussade, Jean-Pierre. *The Sacrament of the Present Moment*.

Paris: Desclee De Brouwer, 1966.

Dentan, Robert C. *The Knowledge of God in Ancient Israel.* New York: Seaburg Press, 1968.

Dürckheim, Karlfried Graf. *The Way of Transformation: Daily Life as Spiritual Exercise.* London: Allen Unwin, 1977.

_____. *Hara: The Vital Center of Man.* London: Mandala Books, 1984.

Eliade, Mircea. Myths, *Dreams and Mysteries.* Translated by Philip Mairet. New York: Harper and Brothers, 1960.

_____. *Myth and Reality.* Translated by Willard R. Trask. New York: Harper and Row, 1963.

Eliade, Mircea and Kitagawa, Joseph M., eds. *The History of Religions: Essays in Methodology.* Chicago: University of Chicago Press, 1959.

Gaster, Theodor H. Myth, *Legend, and Custom in Old Testament Times.* Vol. 1. New York: Harper and Row, 1975.

_____. Thespis: *Ritual, Myth, and Drama in the Ancient Near East.* New York: W.W. Norton and Company, Inc., 1977.

Goettmann, Alphonse. *Dialogue on the Path of Initiation: An Introduction to the Life and Thought of Karlfried Graf Dürckheim.* New York: Globe Press Books, 1992.

_____. *The Beyond Within.* St Meinrad: Abbey Press, 1992.

_____. *Where Silence Dwells: Christian Wisdom and Practice.* Unpublished manuscript.

_____. *Le Chemin*, vol. 15. Béthanie: Editions Béthanie, 1992.

Goguel, Maurice. *The Birth of Christianity*. New York: The Macmillan Company, 1954.

Grou, Jean-Nicholas. *How to Pray*. Greenwood: The Attic Press, 1982.

Gurdjieff, G. I. *Views From the Real World*. New York: E. P. Dutton, 1975.

_____. *Life Is Real Only Then When "I Am"*. New York: E. P. Dutton, 1981.

Higgins, John J. *Thomas Merton on Prayer*. New York: Image Books, 1975.

Jacobsen, Thorkild. *The Treasures of Darkness*. New Haven: Yale University Press, 1976.

James, Fleming. *Personalities of the Old Testament*. New York: Charles Scribner's Sons, 1949.

Jung, C. G. and Kerenyi, C. *Essays on Science and Mythology*. Translated by R.F.C. Hull. Revised edition. New York: Harper Torchbooks, 1963.

Kadloubovsky, E. and Palmer, G. E. H., trans. *Writings from the Philokalia on Prayer of the Heart*. London: Faber and Faber, 1979.

Kelly, Thomas. *A Testament of Devotion*. New York: Harper & Row, 1941.

_____. *Reality of the Spiritual World*. Wallingford: Pendle Hill, 1942.

Kirk, G. S. *Myth: Its Meaning and Functions in Ancient and other Cultures*. Berkeley: University of California Press, 1970.

Knudson, Albert C. *The Prophetic Movement in Israel*. New

York: Abingdon Press, 1966.

Kramer, Samuel N., ed. *Mythologies of the Ancient World.* Garden City, New York: Doubleday and Company, Inc. 1961.

LeFevre, Perry, ed. *Understandings of Prayer.* Philadelphia: The Westminster Press, 1981.

Lindblom, J. *Prophecy in Ancient Israel.* Oxford: Basil Blackwell, 1962.

Loew, Cornelius. *Myth, Sacred History, and Philosophy.* New York: Harcourt, Brace and World, Inc., 1967.

Margueron, Jean-Claude. *Mesopotamia.* Translated by H.S.B. Harrison. New York: The World Publishing Company, 1965.

Merton, Thomas. *New Seeds of Contemplation.* Toronto: New Directions, 1961.

_____. *No Man Is An Island.* New York: Image Books, 1967.

_____. *The Climate of Monastic Prayer.* Kalamazoo: Cistercian Publications, 1981.

_____. *Seasons of Celebration.* New York: Farrar, Straus and Giroux, 1965.

_____. *Love and Living.* New York: Bantam Books, 1979.

Meyer, F. B. *Jeremiah: Priest and Prophet.* London: Morgan and Scott, n.d.

Morgan, G. Campbell. *Studies in the Prophecy of Jeremiah.* New York: Fleming H. Revell Company, 1931.

Naranjo, Claudio and Ornstein Robert E. *On the Psychology of*

Meditation. New York: Viking Press, 1971.

Needleman, Jacob. *Lost Christianity.* New York: Bantam Books, 1982.

Nicoll, Maurice. *Psychological Commentaries on the Teachings of Gurdjieff and Ouspensky.* London: Robinson & Watkins, 1972

_____. *The Mark.* London: Watkings, 1981.

_____. *The New Man.* New York: Penguin Books, 1979.

Nouwen, Henri J. *The Way of the Heart.* New York: The Seabury Press, 1981.

Ouspensky, P. D. *In Search of the Miraculous.* New York: Harcourt Brace Jovanovich, 1977.

_____. *The Psychology of Man's Possible Evolution.* New York: Vintage Books, 1974.

Pedersen, Johs. *Israel: Its Life and Culture.* Vols. 1 and 2. London: Oxford University Press, 1946.

Pennington, M. Basil. *Daily We Touch Him: Practical Religious Experiences.* New York: Image Books, 1977.

_____. "The Many Lives and Stirring Times of Thomas Merton" *National Catholic Reporter* 21 (January 1985).

_____. *Daily We Touch Him.* New York: Image Books, 1977.

Skinner, John. *Prophecy and Religion.* Cambridge: University Press, 1951.

Speeth, Kathleen Riordan. *The Gurdjieff Work.* Berkeley: And/Or Press, 1976.

Steere, Douglas V. *Prayer and Worship.* New York: Harper &

Row, 1938.

_____. *On Beginning from Within*. New York: Harper &
Row, 1943.

Underhill, Evelyn. *Practical Mysticism*. New York: E. P.
Dutton, 1943.

_____. *Worship*. Westport: Hyperion Press, Inc., 1937.

_____. *Concerning the Inner Life*. New York: E. P. Dutton
& Co., Inc., 1926.

_____. *The Mount of Purification*. London: Longmans,
1960.

_____. *Essentials of Mysticism*. New York: E. P. Dutton,
1920.

Johannes Weiss. *Earliest Christianity*. New York: Harper
Torchbooks, 1959.

White, John, ed. *The Highest State of Consciousness*. Garden City:
Anchor Books, 1972.

Woods, Richard, ed. *Understanding Mysticism*. New York:
Image Books, 1980.

Anonymous, *A Guide to True Peace*. New York: Pendle Hill,
1960.